C000095501

LITTLE BOOK OF
CHELTENHAM

LITTLE BOOK OF
CHELTENHAM

First published in the UK in 2014

© G2 Entertainment Limited 2014

www.G2ent.co.uk

ISBN 978-1-782812-51-7

Contents

Foreword

Cheltenham Racecourse holds a very special place in my affections. I remember the tremendous excitement of visits to The Festival as a boy, and my father, Johnny, was instrumental in safeguarding the future of Prestbury Park by founding the Racecourse Holdings Trust, which purchased Cheltenham, in the 1960s. Racecourse Holdings Trust later became Jockey Club Racecourses.

In my time with Fred Winter we had some wonderful days with great horses and I was lucky enough to ride a few winners there as an amateur jockey, although sadly not at The Festival.

The Festival is without doubt the most prestigious fixture of the whole National Hunt season and, not surprisingly, we do target these four special days. It is every owner's dream from the day a horse comes into training to have a runner, let alone a winner, at The Festival. For spectators, punters, jockeys, owners and trainers, Cheltenham is paramount.

I have been lucky enough to train winners there since 1983, starting with See You Then, who helped establish us by winning three Champion Hurdles. We have now had 51 Festival winners – all memorable – and hopefully that is not the end.

Nicky Henderson, August 2014

Introduction: The Magic of Cheltenham

There are 40 racecourses in Britain which hold National Hunt racing. But one towers above the others: Cheltenham. Here, in a natural amphitheatre lying at the foot of the Cotswold hills, nestles the sport's pulsing heart.

Aintree can claim the unique spectacle that is the Grand National. Cheltenham, known as the Home of Jump Racing, however, owns all the class, the prestige and the glory that form the peak of the mountain. This is where every owner, jockey and trainer wants victory. A "Cheltenham winner", be it at the Olympics that is the four-day National Hunt Festival in March, or at one of the course's other seven annual meetings, is an essential strike on their scorecard.

Every single race of the season at the jewel in jump racing's crown is of the highest quality, be it a red-hot handicap hurdle with 20 runners or a novice chase contested by three or four future champions.

Every meeting draws a big, enthusiastic crowd. While some of the fixtures at the major Flat tracks can be beer-fests with the action as a little-noticed side-show, Cheltenham racegoers are knowledgeable and passionate. They come to watch their heroes, equine and human, and to risk the contents of their wallets on their judgement of them.

The atmosphere at The Festival cannot be found anywhere else. It is electric. Fortunes and reputations are made and lost – but the mood of celebration is never dimmed. People are happy at Cheltenham. It has something of the spirit of a bygone age: hats are still sent spiralling high into the air after a popular win; racegoers talk to friend and stranger alike, smiling, keen to share experiences and views.

The significance of winning at The Festival is never seen more clearly than on the face of the greatest jockey of his – or any other – generation, AP McCoy. Bone-white, with eyes sunk as deep as wells, McCoy's despair at being beaten on a fancied horse is palpable. The crowd, standing 10-deep round the winner's enclosure, crammed shoulder to shoulder, will him to win, just to see his face split into a smile and his eyes light up, transformed. He is their god.

Town and country, often poles apart in modern Britain, come together at Cheltenham. Children and pensioners, billionaires and those who had to scrape together the train fare share the same emotions of surging thrill and disappointment. While champagne is certainly consumed in quantities, a hearty, heady pint of Guinness is Cheltenham's drink. A visit to the Guinness Village before racing at The Festival is an annual compulsion, and punters, trainers, bloodstock agents and builders jostle amicably for standing-room.

Cheltenham is all about supreme sport but, while it is nearly impossible for a small team or one-man band to win a top-class Flat race, dreams really can come true at Prestbury Park. David can – and does – defeat Goliath. Witness Welsh farmer Sirrel Griffiths' 1990 Gold Cup triumph with 100-1 shot Norton's Coin. Griffiths milked his cows, drove from Carmarthenshire to Cheltenham, won the race – beating the most popular National Hunt horse of all time, Desert Orchid, and then loaded up his home-bred chestnut, on whom Griffiths used to round up the stock on his farm, and drove back.

It doesn't matter whether not a single member of the crowd has had a penny on the winner at The Festival – the returning conqueror is still cheered in with respect and appreciation.

But when the favourites for the championship races do their stuff, the bellow nearly blows the roof off the grandstand. "We were right," it seems to say. "This is a great horse."

An integral part of Cheltenham's special atmosphere is the fact that National Hunt horses' career last for several seasons. Flat racing's endgame is a stud career, and the best horses race for a scant two, or possibly three, seasons. Jumping is different – it is all about the racing itself – and its equine characters return year after year for a tilt at the mill. They become characters,

Above: *racegoers watch the action from the Grandstand on Gold Cup Day at Cheltenham Racecourse*

rather than ciphers, and we take them, with their talents and their foibles, to our hearts.

There are the scintillating champions, like Kauto Star, Big Buck's and Sprinter Sacre. Then there are the less-talented but equally big-hearted old friends like the David Pipe-trained Buena Vista, who ran an amazing eight times in succession at The Festival and twice won the Pertemps Final. The expansion of The Festival from three days to four in 2005 may have very slightly blunted its razor-sharp quality, but it has extended its inclusivity and lost none of its extreme competiveness.

Even Flat jockeys can't resist its lure; Jamie Spencer sneaked a win on Pizarro in the 2002 Champion Bumper – a race which has also featured Richard Hughes, Kieren Fallon, Pat Smullen and Joseph O'Brien, among others. And Johnny Murtagh came within inches of winning the 2006 World Hurdle on Golden Cross, going down to Robert Thornton and My Way De Solzen by a head.

The Irish have a special relationship with Cheltenham. More than 10,000 of them make the trip over for The Festival – Ryanair puts on an extra 30 flights between Dublin and Birmingham that week – but you'd think they made up at least half of the 50,000-strong crowd.

St Patrick's Day usually falls during the meeting, giving anyone with a drop of Irish blood further excuse for rip-roaring celebrations.

Irish trainers followed the great Vincent O'Brien's lead in plundering Cheltenham's prizes after the Second World War, and their participation has been a vital ingredient in The Festival's intoxicating recipe ever since. Irish punters back their domestic heroes with emotional fervour and pride. A half-serious "Britain v Ireland" competition pervades – now formalised at The Festival in the shape of the Prestbury Cup, and each clan member hopes that, if their horse can't win, that of another compatriot will. Many Irish racing fans treat their visits to Cheltenham as pilgrimages to worship at the altar of jump racing.

While racing fans are often happy to watch Royal Ascot on the television, they feel they must attend Cheltenham. They feel the charge of history; young men born long after Arkle can recite the precise details of his achievements, while old men are stirred to tears by the remembered sounds of Sir Peter

O'Sullevan's commentaries.

The multi-talented John Hislop, amateur jockey, journalist and owner-breeder of the exceptional Flat racehorse Brigadier Gerard, wrote in his book *Steeplechasing*:

"Steeplechasing has about it rather more glamour and excitement than the Flat, a trace of chivalry, a spice of danger, and a refreshing vigor that the smooth urbanity of Flat racing lacks. The atmosphere is less restrained, more friendly, more intimate and more sympathetic."

The description applies to the whole of National Hunt racing – and nowhere more so than at Cheltenham, the sport's Mecca.

National Hunt Racing Explained

National Hunt racing is the name given to the type of racing where horses jump obstacles during contests. It is split into two main parts: hurdling, over brush fences around 3ft 6in high, and steeplechasing, over bigger brushes obstacles around 4ft 6in high, some with small ditches in front. Most steeplechasing tracks also feature a water jump.

Races are run over distances between two miles and 4½ miles.

There are also National Hunt Flat races, known as "bumpers", which are confined to young horses which have not run under Flat Rules and which are used to educate them in preparation for a career over jumps.

Cheltenham is the only course in Britain to contain a special "Cross-Country Course", where horses jump a variety of different obstacles. Cheltenham has joined with other racecourses across Europe in the Crystal Cup – a series of valuable cross-country races which encourage participants to compete internationally and which climax at Cheltenham in December.

Britain, Ireland and France are jump racing's strongholds, although the sport does take place in countries such as the USA, Japan, New Zealand, Australia, Germany, Sweden, Norway and the Czech Republic as well.

The First Century

If you drive away from Cheltenham Racecourse to the north, along the A435 towards Evesham, after a couple of miles you pass a small hill on your right. This is Nottingham Hill, and it was here, on a grassy crest flattened by Iron Age earthworks, that the first Cheltenham race-meeting was held in 1815.

By 1818, a more formal event, with five races, was staged on nearby Cleeve Hill. And in 1819, three days of racing climaxed with the inaugural running of the Cheltenham Gold Cup.

The 68,000 people who watch the modern-day Gold Cup would be unmoved by the 1819 renewal. It was a three-mile Flat race without a fence in sight, and Mr Bodenham's Spectre claimed the 100-guinea prize.

Cheltenham was a deeply fashionable spa town, first popularised by King George III in 1788 when he visited with his family to take the waters in an attempt to alleviate the mental health problems that dogged his reign. A succession of well-heeled visitors followed him, and the races became a popular entertainment. As many as 50,000 people may have attended the 1825 meeting.

Racing at Cheltenham suffered a dip in its fortunes after a local clergyman, Francis Close – later Dean Close, after whom a public school in the town is named - campaigned vociferously against its evil influence. His adherents badly

Did You Know...?

That Cheltenham's first clerk of the course was Frederick Cathcart? He was clerk and chairman from 1908-1934, and was largely responsible for developing it into Britain's leading National Hunt track. For many years, the Cathcart Challenge Cup was run at The Festival in his memory.

Did You Know...?

That Dick Rees, who rode Red Splash to win the first Cheltenham Gold Cup as we know it in 1924, won the race twice more – in 1928 on Patron Saint and in 1930 on Easter Hero? The Welshman was the first National Hunt jockey to win more than 100 races in a season (1924), and also won a Champion Hurdle (Royal Falcon in 1929) and a Grand National (Shaun Spadhu in 1921).

disrupted the 1829 meeting and in 1830 burnt the grandstand down.

The Cleeve Hill site was abandoned for a few years, and in 1831 the Tory politician Lord Ellenborough, later Governor-General of India, allowed his land at Prestbury Park to be used for racing for the first time. A stand that could accommodate 700 people was erected and a horse called Confederacy won the first race, the Gloucestershire Stakes, on 19 July 1831.

Further meetings did take place on Cleeve Hill, but Francis Close's preachings had had their effect and Flat racing at Cheltenham petered out in the 1840s.

But the less smart sport of steeplechasing, which was born out of the hunting field, was beginning to take root. The village of Andoversford hosted Gloucestershire's first properly organised race over fences in April 1834, and subsequently became known as the Grand Annual Steeplechase – still run at The Festival today.

LITTLE BOOK OF **CHELTENHAM**

In 1854 Prestbury Park changed hands and the new incumbent stopped racing on the site. Meetings were still held on various sites round the town, such as Andoversford and Kayte Farm in Southam – Kaytes Lane is now a popular "rat-run" for those hoping to escape the heavy traffic that inevitably develops around The Festival – and in 1866 the grandstand there collapsed and decanted spectators into the refreshment room below.

Interest in jump racing flagged all over the country in the later part of Queen Victoria's reign, and there were few significant meetings held except for the Grand National. But help was at hand: Mr Baring Bingham bought Prestbury Park in the 1880s, rebuilt the grandstand, put rails up on the course and held a race-meeting in 1898. The course began to take on the shape we all recognise today and four years later in 1902, a two-day meeting was held on 9-10 April and The

Opposite: *Brown Jack, who took the 1928 Champion Hurdle before going on to become a multiple Royal Ascot winner, with jockey Steve Donoghue*

Cheltenham's First Equine Hero

Brown Jack, who won the second ever running of the Champion Hurdle in 1928, became one of the most popular horses in racing history. It wasn't his exploits over the sticks that earned him fame, however – it was his extraordinary record at Royal Ascot, where he took the Queen Alexandra Stakes, Britain's longest Flat race at 2¾ miles – six times in succession.

Trained by first Aubrey Hastings and then Jack Anthony, Brown Jack was owned by Sir Harold Wernher. He won seven hurdles races in his first season as a four-year-old, including the Champion Hurdle, then switched to the Flat.

Brown Jack took the Ascot Stakes at the Royal meeting in 1928, just a couple of months after his Champion Hurdle victory, and became a standing dish at Ascot, winning the Queen Alexandra each year from 1929-1934. He also won the Goodwood Cup, the Doncaster Cup, the Chester Cup and the Ebor Handicap. A beautiful bronze of the horse by Munnings can be seen at Ascot, and a race bearing his name is run at the track's May meeting.

Festival at Cheltenham came alive.

In 1860, the National Hunt Committee had been formed and the National Hunt Steeplechase was founded. This race formed part of a race-meeting staged at a different track each year, and in 1904 and 1905 Cheltenham hosted the event. Although Warwick then took it on for five years, it then made its permanent home at Cheltenham and grew into the March meeting around which the National Hunt season pivots.

The Steeplechase Company was formed in 1908, and a building programme steadily introduced new additions to the course each year.

However, in 1914 the First World War broke out. A few days' racing took place in 1915, but Cheltenham's principal use during the Great War was as a Red Cross troop hospital. More than 3,000 cases were treated between October 1914 and February 1919.

Racing resumed in the spring of 1919, and thousands flocked to the course. After the horrors of the past five years, the feeling of relief at returning to "normality" must have been immense.

The Festival was extended from two days to three in 1923, and remained that length until 2005, when it increased to four days, Tuesday-Friday. The Gold Cup, then, as it is now, a steeplechase over 3¼ miles, was introduced in 1925,

The Archer Family

Cheltenham has a strong link with one of the most famous Flat jockeys of the 19th century. Fred Archer, who was champion jockey for 13 consecutive seasons, was born in Prestbury in 1857. His father William went to Russia aged 17, where he managed Tsar Nicholas I's stud before returning home to Gloucestershire to run the King's Arms pub in Prestbury. Fred's brothers William and Charles were jump jockeys – sadly William was killed in a fall at Cheltenham in 1878, eight years before Fred took his own life at the age of 29. Charles Archer perpetuated the family's racing tradition, however, and trained the 1925 Grand National winner, Double Chance.

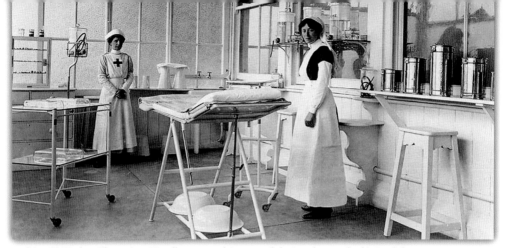

and in 1927 the Champion Hurdle was added to the card.

The first horse to be acclaimed as the Cheltenham Gold Cup winner was Red Splash, owned by Major Everard Wyndham and trained by Fred Withington. Aged five, Red Splash was the youngest horse in the race, but he made all the running under Dick Rees to win the £685 first prize, just beating Conjuror II and Gerald L.

Former champion jockey George Duller, a hurdles specialist, rode Blaris to take the first Champion Hurdle. Trained by Bill Payne and sent off the 11-10 favourite, six-year-old Blaris had just three rivals to see off to win his £365 prize. Duller later turned to motor racing and became one of the first professional drivers, and during the war had joined the Royal Flying Corps.

The following year, 1928, the Champion Hurdle went to Brown Jack, who went on to greater things on the Flat. It was in this decade, the "Roaring Twenties", that National Hunt racing started to catch up with its older, more sophisticated cousin, the Flat game. Greater prize-money attracted richer owners, and trainers and jockeys became more professional in their approach.

Easter Hero was perhaps the first chaser really to catch the public's imagination and he made his mark at Cheltenham in 1929. He won the Gold Cup that year and the next, both times by more than 20 lengths. He had true class, and could be claimed to be the first great chaser.

Above:
Cheltenham Racecourse became a Voluntary Aid (VA) hospital during the Second World War

Opposite: *Easter Hero and Tommy Cullinan, 1930 Cheltenham Gold Cup winners*

Irish-bred Easter Hero was by the brilliant jumps sire My Prince, also responsible for dual Grand National winner Reynoldstown and Gold Cup winner Prince Regent. The handsome horse changed owners and trainers several times before being bought by Belgian financier Capt Alfred Lowenstein for the enormous sum of £7,000 – plus a £3,000 contingency should he win his first target, the 1928 Grand National. He didn't, falling at the open ditch at the Canal Turn, and soon afterwards his owner disappeared when his plane went missing over the North Sea.

A rich American, John "Jock" Hay Whitney, bought Easter Hero for £11,000 and sent him to be trained by Jack Anthony at Letcombe Regis. Anthony, who had been champion jockey in 1914 and 1928, produced the horse to win four times over hurdles before heading to Cheltenham for the Gold Cup. He won in a canter, ridden by Dick Rees, who had won the previous year's race on Patron Saint.

Tommy Cullinan rode him in 1930, when he beat Grakle, ridden by Lester Piggott's father Keith.

He missed out in 1931, when the race was cancelled due to bad weather, and was retired. His owner, John "Jock" Hay Whitney, US Ambassador to the Court of St James, took him home to America and hunted him for several seasons in Virginia. He finally died aged 28 in 1948.

Brown Jack and Easter Hero ushered in a new era at Cheltenham; the Grand National might remain a thrilling spectacle, but the best horses, those with talent and class, excelled at Prestbury Park.

Winning-most jockeys in the Gold Cup

Pat Taaffe: 4 (Arkle 1964-66, Fort Leney 1968)
Aubrey Brabazon: 3 (Cottage Rake 1948-50)
Tommy Carberry: 3 (L'Escargot 1970-71, Ten Up 1975)
Jim Culloty: 3 (Best Mate 2002-04)
Dick Rees: 3 (Red Splash 1924, Patron Saint 1928, Easter Hero 1929)

The Age of Golden Miller and Cottage Rake

It is a tribute to the race's championship status that just seven horses have won the Cheltenham Gold Cup more than once. Three horses have won it three times; only one has triumphed five times.

It seems highly unlikely that any horse will ever seize Golden Miller's record, carved out between 1932 and 1936, from him. There are only two real claimants for the title of the finest steeplechaser of the 20th century. And while Arkle's supporters will maintain that the three-times champion takes it on the grounds of sheer brilliance, the counter-argument is that "The Miller"'s record says it all – and that he won a Grand National, too.

Basil Briscoe, who trained Golden Miller for most of his career, bought him unseen as a three-year-old from the Leicestershire bloodstock dealer Dick Farmer, who found him in Ireland. The well-bred, gangly colt was first sold to one of Briscoe's owners, Philip Carr, in 1930 for £1,000 and won a couple of hurdle races for him.

But Carr discovered he was terminally ill and in 1931 Briscoe sold Golden Miller again. The Hon Dorothy Paget, whose interest in racing had been sparked by her cousin Jock Whitney's successes with Easter Hero, paid £10,000 for him and another horse, Insurance.

Briscoe promised Paget she was buying the best chaser and the best hurdler in England. Many trainers have made such statements to prospective

owners; in this case, it proved to be true.

Golden Miller won three out of his first four races in Paget's blue and yellow silks, but the five-year-old wasn't favourite for his first Gold Cup in 1932. That honour went to Grakle, who had won the previous year's Grand National. In the race, Grakle unseated his jockey and Golden Miller, ridden by Ted Leader, won comfortably. A couple of hours later, Insurance took the Champion Hurdle and Briscoe went

home to Cambridgeshire a happy man.

In 1933, under Billy Stott, Golden Miller strode away to win the race by 10 lengths. For good measure, Insurance doubled up again in the Champion Hurdle.

The press and public had been slow to warm to Golden Miller, who lacked Easter Hero's glittering presence and whose jumping was more economical than spectacular. But it couldn't be denied that he was a very good horse, and his exploits the following year were to cement him as a national hero.

This time Gerry Wilson was on board, and the pair saw off challenger after challenger en route to a six-length victory. But Briscoe and Paget's real target that year was Aintree and, carrying 12st 2lb, Golden Miller caught Delaneige after the final fence to take the Grand National.

Now he made newspaper headlines and the Sporting Life acclaimed him the "Finest chaser of the century".

That 1934 renewal was the only Grand National he would win, despite contesting it several times. Golden Miller's place to shine was Cheltenham, and he did so again in 1935. Only five horses lined up for that year's Gold Cup, but it turned into an epic contest between two of them, attracting vast crowds.

Jock Whitney's excellent chaser Thomond II had come up against The Miller several times, beating him once at Kempton. The two horses settled at the back together this time at Cheltenham, content to let Southern Hero make the pace.

But, with less than a mile to go, both jockeys – Gerry Wilson on Golden Miller and Billy Speck on Thomond II – stepped on the accelerator. The two horses raced each other flat out, leaving their rivals trailing, jumping with such stunning accuracy and boldness that the overexcited spectators were cheering their heads off before they got to the final fence. Golden Miller landed over it an inch in front, and held his marginal lead up the hill, winning by three-quarters of a length.

It was a breath-taking effort by both horses and both jockeys, and Golden Miller's greatest performance.

The two horses went to Aintree a fortnight later, but neither could replicate their Cheltenham heroics. The

Multiple Gold Cup Winners

Golden Miller: 5
Arkle: 3
Best Mate: 3
Cottage Rake: 3
Easter Hero: 2
L'Escargot: 2
Kauto Star: 2

capricious Paget took her horses away from Briscoe, and it was Owen Anthony who prepared Golden Miller for a fifth Cheltenham Gold Cup in 1936.

Anthony, who had already won the 1927 Gold Cup with Thrown In and whose brother Jack had trained Easter Hero, was well up to the task. Ridden this time by Evan Williams, who later became master and huntsman of the Tipperary Foxhounds in Ireland, Golden Miller produced the old magic and took the race by 12 lengths from Royal Mail.

There is every chance Golden Miller would have won a sixth Gold Cup if the 1937 race hadn't been lost to flooding. By the time 1938 came around, the great horse's legs didn't enjoy the unusually firm ground the race was run on and he went down, despite a heroic attempt, to Morse Code by two lengths.

Given the fragile nature of the thoroughbred and the extremes to which their hearts, limbs and joints are pushed, it is a feat to win one race at Cheltenham. To prevail in five Gold Cups is like winning five Olympic gold medals, and Golden Miller deserves to be counted among the greatest athletes of all time – in any sport.

Golden Miller shared his retirement with Insurance – remember that promise Basil Briscoe made to Dorothy Paget? He lived until the age of 30, dreaming of past glories at Cheltenham.

The 1939 Gold Cup – won by Brendan's Cottage – paled into significance very quickly beside other events that year. War raged round Europe by its close, and racing took a backseat in people's minds.

Evan Williams rode another Gold Cup winner, Roman Hackle, for Dorothy Paget in 1940 and the race was run in both 1941 and 1942, but the programme was much reduced round the country and suspended from September 1942 until the end of hostilities.

This time the racecourse served as a training camp for troops, first British and then American. The 1945 Festival was a two-day meeting, and the Gold Cup went to Red Rower, bred, owned and trained by Lord Stalbridge.

It took a few years for another truly great horse to inscribe his name into Cheltenham's annals. At the end of the 1940s, two came along at once. One was a hurdler – Hatton's Grace – and one was a chaser – Cottage Rake. Both were trained by an Irishman – Vincent O'Brien.

Cottage Rake, by the top-class sire Cottage, didn't have the start in life one imagines of a champion. He failed pre-purchase veterinary inspections three times before O'Brien persuaded Frank Vickerman to buy him, and it took a while for his racing career to get into gear. But in 1947 Cottage Rake won the Irish Cesarewitch, a famous handicap on the Flat, and went to Cheltenham to raid the Gold Cup for the first time in March 1948.

Aubrey Brabazon rode him to victory, and repeated the feat in the next two Gold Cups. Their exploits are celebrated in verse:

> "Aubrey's up, the money's down
> The frightened bookies quake
> Come on, my lads, and give a cheer
> Begod, 'tis Cottage Rake!"

O'Brien is quoted as saying, "Cottage Rake was not a robust horse and could not give weight away like Arkle, but he had something special; there were very few chasers who had speed after jumping the last."

Cottage Rake's Gold Cup treble was just the start of O'Brien's remarkable achievements in racing. In 1949, a

horse he had bought for just 1,800 guineas, Hatton's Grace, took the first of three Champion Hurdles. Aubrey Brabazon rode him for the first two and Tim Molony took over for the last, in 1951. Hatton's Grace was 11 when he flew across the winning line in 1951 – only Sea Pigeon, in the second of his two wins in the race in 1981, has been as old.

O'Brien trained one more Gold Cup winner, Knock Hard in 1953, and three Grand National winners (Early Mist in 1953, Royal Tan in 1954, Quare Times in 1955) before moving from Churchtown in Co Cork to Ballydoyle

Tim Molony

Born in Limerick in 1919, Tim Molony is still the only jockey to win four Champion Hurdles, having taken the 1951 race on Hatton's Grace and the next three on Sir Ken. He also won a Gold Cup on Knock Hard and was champion jockey five times. He never won a Grand National, but plays a curious footnote in the Aintree race's history. He bought Red Rum as a yearling and trained him to win a selling race at Aintree in 1967, six years before the horse's first of three National victories in the hands of Ginger McCain.

in Co Tipperary. He turned his attention to the Flat, in which sphere he was to win 27 Classic races, including six Derbys.

O'Brien is generally considered to be the greatest racehorse trainer of all time. But it all started with Cottage Rake – and Cheltenham, where he trained 23 winners between 1948 and 1959.

Given how rare repeat winners of championship races are, it is remarkable that, immediately after Hatton's Grace's domination, another top-class hurdler should sweep up the Cheltenham hill and take three Champion Hurdles.

Trained in Hertfordshire by Willie Stephenson, Sir Ken was unbeaten in two seasons over hurdles before he took on – and beat – an ageing Hatton's Grace in the Champion Hurdle in 1952. His run of success continued to span 17 races, including a second Champion Hurdle.

But the hugely popular star caused a shock in November 1953 when he was beaten – at odds of 1-7 – by Impney, trained locally by Phil Doherty on Cleeve Hill. No one really imagined Impney could best Sir Ken again at Cheltenham in 1954, and the horses were priced up at 9-1 and 4-9 respectively. However, the younger horse led over the last hurdle and, in a desperate duel up the hill, Sir Ken only just got his nose in front with half a furlong to go. He had won his third Champion Hurdle in thrilling style.

The Mighty Men of Cheltenham

Opposite: *Fortria and Pat Taaffe lead eventual winners Fred Winter and Mandarin in the 1962 Cheltenham Gold Cup*

"They don't make 'em how they used to." It's an often-repeated phrase, but it could have been designed to fit three men whose influence on Cheltenham was unparalleled in the middle decades of the 20th century.

Fred Winter and Fred Rimell both achieved the singular honour of becoming not only champion jockey, but later champion trainer as well. Fulke Walwyn won the Grand National as an amateur jockey on Reynoldstown, and went on to train 40 winners at The Festival – a record that stood until Nicky Henderson topped it in 2012. They were jumping men to the bone.

Winter, who was born in 1926 and died in 2004, was born into a racing family and rode his first winner for his father Fred snr, who was training in Epsom at the time, at Salisbury in 1940. He rode two further winners before joining the army and serving in Palestine, returning to civilian life in 1947.

Now too heavy to ride on the Flat, he turned to jumping. He rode his first winner under National Hunt Rules for his father at Kempton on Boxing Day that year. A serious accident incurred when racing at the now-defunct Wye meant he was out of action for some time, but by the end of the 1952-53 season he was champion jockey for the first time.

A further three titles followed, from 1955 to 1958, and he rode the

winners of all the major races, mostly for trainer Capt Ryan Price. Winter took Champion Hurdles with Clair Soleil in 1955 and Fare Time in 1957, a brace of Triumph Hurdles with Clair Soleil (1953) and Cantab (1961) and more than a dozen other races at The Festival. For good measure, he rode the winner of the Grand National twice as well – on Sundew in 1957 and Kilmore in 1962.

His first Gold Cup winner came in 1961, on the Don Butchers-trained Saffron Tartan. It is for his partnership with Mandarin, trained by Fulke Walwyn, however, that Winter's name will live on.

They scored in the 1962 Gold Cup, and went on to Paris three months later for the Grand Steeplechase de Paris at Auteuil. Disastrously, Mandarin's bit broke in half at the fourth fence, leaving Winter with no brakes and no steering. In an extraordinary display of skill and horsemanship – helped by his fellow jockeys, who made no attempt to take advantage of the situation – Mandarin still won the race.

The amateur jockey and journalist Lord Oaksey wrote in *Horse & Hound*: "I have never seen a comparable feat, never expect to – and can only thank God I was there."

Winter retired from riding in 1964 with 929 winners – and a strike-rate of almost one in four. He started training at Uplands stables in Lambourn, and was immediately out of the starting stalls, winning the Grand National twice in his first two seasons, first with Jay Trump and then with Anglo.

He took the trainers' championship in 1971, the year of his first of two consecutive Champion Hurdle triumphs with Bula. Lanzarote followed up in the 1974 race, while Crisp gave him a Queen Mother Champion Chase in 1971.

Midnight Court was his – and John Francome's – only Gold Cup victory, in 1978. But there were other big wins with the likes of dual Festival winner Soloning, Derring Rose (1981 Stayers' Hurdle), Half Free, who won at The Festival in 1984, 1986 and 1987, Pendil (1972 Arkle) and Venture To Cognac.

Winter's last Festival winner was Celtic Shot in the 1988 Champion Hurdle, and he retired in June that year following a severe stroke, handing over the reins to Charlie Brooks, who had ridden him a Foxhunter victory on Observe in 1987. He was champion trainer eight times in total.

Lester Piggott & Sir Henry Cecil

Two of Flat racing's greatest legends can claim to have won races at The Festival.

Lester Piggott, who rode 20 winners over hurdles in the early part of his career, won the 1954 Triumph Hurdle on Prince Charlemagne – a couple of months before he took the Derby on Never Say Die, the first of his nine victories in the Epsom Classic.

Sir Henry Cecil's success was a less formal one. In 2011 the 10-times champion trainer saddled Plato to win Cheltenham's St Patrick's Day Derby, a charity race run in aid of Cancer Research UK, ridden by Lorna Fowler.

In an obituary in the *Guardian*, Julian Wilson wrote: "Throughout his life, he was admired for his integrity, resolution and fierce determination to win."

Fred Rimell was Winter's senior by 13 years. He was another to ride his first winner for his trainer father – aged 12, at Chepstow – and managed 33 winners on the Flat before switching to the National Hunt scene.

Among his successes in a riding career that included three jockeys' titles was a Champion Hurdle on Brains Trust in 1945. But a fall on Coloured Schoolboy in the 1947 Gold Cup, in which he broke his neck for the second time, saw him switch to training.

He had actually taken out a licence in 1945, taking over from his father Tom at Kinnersley in Worcestershire. He was the first trainer to earn his owners £1million in prize-money, adding his name to nearly every big-race trophy on offer.

There were four Grand Nationals – ESB in 1956, Nicolaus Silver in 1961, Gay Trip in 1970 and Rag Trade in 1976. Rimell's two Gold Cups, with Woodland Venture and Royal Frolic, were just two of his 27 Festival winners. He trained the great hurdler Comedy Of Errors, to Champion Hurdle success in 1973 and 1975, losing out to Fred Winter's Lanzarote in between.

Rimell's wife Mercy, who took over the training licence when he died in 1981, kept Comedy Of Errors as her hack for many years after the horse's retirement.

The third member of this triumvirate, Fulke Walwyn, trained next door to Winter in Lambourn. He bought Saxon House Stables in 1944, and became champion trainer for the first time in 1947. He lost the title in 1949, but regained it in 1958 and again in 1964.

His initial Festival triumph arrived in 1946's Grand Annual with Loyal King – ridden by Dan Moore, later to become a great trainer himself. In 1948 Jean's Last took the second division of the Gloucestershire Hurdle – a race he was

to win three more times – and On View won the Broadway Novices' Chase. A year later he took the Kim Muir with Jack Tatters, ridden by Lord Mildmay. Both jockey and trainer were later to give their names to races at The Festival – Walwyn's to that very race, making it the Fulke Walwyn Kim Muir Challenge Cup.

In 1956 Michael Scudamore rode him the winner of the Triumph Hurdle, Square Dance.

There were back-to-back Arkle Chases with Amorial III and Manuscrit in the 1950s; three Stayers' Hurdles, two with Crimson Embers and one with Rose Ravine – who controversially beat her stable-mate Crimson Embers in the

Did You Know…?

That "Frenchie" Nicholson was so called because he was apprenticed to a French trainer in Chantilly while his father hunted the Pau Foxhounds in the very south of France? His real name was Herbert.

Did You Know…?

That £150million is bet on The Festival every year?

David Nicholson

He may not have trained quite as many Festival winners – "just" 17 – but David Nicholson was the spiritual heir to Walwyn, Winter and Rimell.

Son of "Frenchie" Nicholson, a successful trainer and winner of the Gold Cup aboard Medoc II in 1948, David was nicknamed "The Duke", supposedly for his somewhat imperious manner. He rode more than 600 winners between 1951 and 1974, including the 1968 Whitbread Gold Cup on Mill House and the 1971 Queen Mother Champion Chase on Tantalum, and took out a training licence in 1969, combining the two careers for five years.

It was a source of frustration that, training locally to Cheltenham at Condicote, it took him 17 years to score at The Festival. But the winners did come: the Gold Cup with Charter Party in 1988; Triumph Hurdles with Solar Cloud and Mysliv; the Queen Mother Champion Chase in 1994 and 1995 courtesy of Viking Flagship; the Stayers' Hurdle with Anzum, to name a few.

He moved to the purpose-built Jackdaws Castle near Naunton in 1992 – now inhabited by Jonjo O'Neill – and he was twice champion trainer from there in the 1990s.

He was an unmistakable figure at Cheltenham in his sheepskin coat and trilby, and held trenchant views on a variety of subjects. But he was utterly devoted to the sport of National Hunt racing and wore his heart on his sleeve, which endeared him to the general public.

Nicholson, who was responsible for starting the careers of a fleet of jockeys such as Richard Dunwoody – who rode Charter Party – Peter Scudamore, Adrian Maguire, Richard Johnson and Robert Thornton, died in 2006. His widow Dinah is still a regular visitor to Cheltenham.

1985 race, and most of the other Festival races were added to his score-sheet at some point.

His first Gold Cup came in 1952 with Mont Tremblant, ridden by Dave Dick and owned by the eccentric Dorothy Paget. Mandarin gave him another – and The Dikler did so again in 1973.

The name that strikes a chord with the present generation of racegoers, though, is that of Mill House. The 18hh Irish-bred with the looks of a champion show horse was considered one of the "best of all time" after his 1963 Gold Cup success – but then he met Arkle (see page 42).

Walwyn, cousin of the well-known Flat trainer Peter, grabbed a pair of Champion Hurdles with Anzio in 1962 and Kirriemuir in 1965, but never managed a Queen Mother Champion Chase – although he did train for the lady herself. His final Festival winner was Ten Plus, who took the Royal & SunAlliance Hurdle in 1986. He retired as a titan of National Hunt racing that year with just about every great British race to his name, including a Grand National, seven Hennessy Gold Cups and five King George VI Chases. He died in 1991.

Hurdling's 'Golden Age'

The 1970s were the golden age of hurdling; to extend it a year or two either side of the decade encompasses most of the greatest horses ever to jump a flight.

Persian War heralded the era in. His remarkable career included five changes of trainer due to the quixotic demands of his owner, Henry Alper, and it is thought that he could achieved even more under less erratic ownership.

Brian Swift trained him to Triumph Hurdle success in 1967, but Welshman Colin Davies was asked to take over after that and rescued the horse from France, where he found him "freezing cold and sick."

Davies nursed him back to health and secured a first Champion Hurdle – by four lengths – in 1968 with him, beating former winners Saucy Kit and Salmon Spray on fast ground. A second followed in 1969, again by four lengths in very testing going.

Alper insisted Persian War ran on the Flat, too, and he jarred himself up on firm ground at Newbury, to his trainer's despair. But Davies still managed to win a third Champion Hurdle the following March, this time by a length and a half from Major Rose.

Sadly, despite Davies' terrific success with the horse, Alper removed him from his yard in the summer of 1970 and sent him to Arthur Pitt in Epsom. Pitt won three races with Persian War, but

the great horse's best days were behind him. Switching yards again, this time to Dennis Rayson and later Jack Gibson, he eventually retired in 1974 aged 11. It was an ignominious end to the career of one of the best hurdlers ever to have set foot on a racecourse.

Persian War conceded his crown in 1971 to Bula, whom Fred Winter trained to a second success in 1972. Bula

turned his hoof to chasing after handing the baton to Comedy Of Errors, who took the 1973 and 1975 races.

Then came Night Nurse. Peter Easterby bought the Irish-bred son of Falcon as a yearling for just 1,100 guineas, and said when the much-loved horse died aged 27 in 1999, "What made Night Nurse so special was he was a natural jumper, brilliant from the first

time we ever schooled him. He was a very, very brave horse, hard and brave."

Easterby sold him to Reg Spencer, whose pink and purple colours Night Nurse made famous, just before he won his first race at Market Rasen as a four-year-old. In the 1975-76 season he was unbeaten, taking the Champion Hurdle and its equivalents in Ireland, Scotland and Wales.

Did You Know...?

That dual Champion Hurdle winner Monksfield sired Its A Snip, who in 1995 became only the second British horse ever to win the Velka Pardubice in the Czech Republic?

Did You Know...?

That Jonjo O'Neill, who won the 1980 Champion Hurdle on Sea Pigeon, also won one of Flat racing's biggest handicaps, the Ebor, on the horse in 1979?

The 1977 Champion Hurdle field was one of the strongest ever assembled, and Night Nurse saw off two horses who themselves would become dual winners of the race – Monksfield and Sea Pigeon – to triumph for a second time under Paddy Broderick.

Night Nurse was third the following year behind Monksfield and Sea Pigeon, and in 1979 went chasing, in which discipline he won some valuable races and finished second to Little Owl in the 1981 Gold Cup.

Monksfield cost even less as a yearling than Night Nurse. His Co Meath trainer Des McDonogh got him for only 740 guineas, and won a maiden on the Flat with him on his racecourse debut.

But hurdling was his game, and as a novice he won four times before finishing second to the Mick Easterby-trained Peterhof in the 1976 Triumph Hurdle.

The Champion Hurdle had to be his target the following season. Ridden by Tommy Kinane – father of the Classic-winning jockey Mick – he couldn't quite get to Night Nurse. A month later at Aintree the two horses dead-heated after a pulsating duel all the way from the second-last hurdle.

A year older and stronger in 1978, little Monksfield galloped gamely through the mud to record his first

Opposite: *Sir Ken, who won the 1952, 1953 and 1954 runnings of the Champion Hurdle for trainer Willie Stephenson and jockey Tim Molony*

Champion Hurdle win over Night Nurse and Sea Pigeon.

He took the Aintree Hurdle again weeks later, and won twice on the Flat before going down by a narrow margin to Royal Gaye in the Swinton Hurdle at Haydock under a huge weight.

The public loved him for his bravery in defeat as well as his many successes, and his 1979 Champion Hurdle win was greeted with wild scenes of celebration. He was collared by Sea Pigeon at the final hurdle, but Monksfield – with Dessie Hughes in the saddle – battled back with tremendous guts to record a narrow success. A third Aintree Hurdle followed.

Rarely for a National Hunt horse, he wasn't gelded and was sent to stand at stud after defeat by Sea Pigeon in the 1980 race. However Dessie Hughes' connection with the Champion Hurdle was far from over – he trained the doughty Hardy Eustace to win the race in 2004 and 2005.

Sea Pigeon rounded off the "golden age", winning the 1980 and 1981 renewals. Trained, like Night Nurse, by Peter Easterby at Habton Grange in North Yorkshire, he was bred in the United States by Jock Whitney.

Sea Pigeon was a son of the magnificent 1965 Derby winner Sea-Bird II and, after winning a stakes race at Ascot in the autumn of his two-year-old year when trained by Jeremy Tree, was considered a Classic contender. He didn't live up to expectations and could

Winning-Most Jockeys in the Champion Hurdle

Tim Molony: 4 (Hatton's Grace 1951, Sir Ken 1952-54)
AP McCoy: 3 (Make A Stand 1997, Brave Inca 2006, Binocular 2010)
Steve Smith Eccles: 3 (See You Then, 1985-87)
Charlie Swan: 3 (Istabraq 1998-2000)
Ron Smyth: 3 (Seneca 1941, Forestation 1942, National Spirit 1948)
Jimmy Uttley: 3 (Persian War 1968-1970)
Fred Winter: 3 (Clair Soleil 1955, Fare Time 1959, Eborneezer 1961)

See You Then

Between Persian War and Istabraq, one other horse took three Champion Hurdles. See You Then put Nicky Henderson on the map as a trainer – his first Champion Hurdle success in 1985 was Henderson's first Festival win – but it was his handling of the fragile horse that proved just how skilful he was.

See You Then's legs only stood up to 15 runs over hurdles, but he won 10 of those. After taking the 1985 Champion Hurdle, he raced just six more times – but two of those were Champion Hurdle victories.

Steve Smith Eccles guided him to a seven-length win in 1985, and the pair triumphed by the same distance from Gaye Brief in 1986. In 1987 he beat the American horse Flatterer – the only four-times winner of that country's Eclipse Award – by a length and a half.

Opposite: *See You Then and Steve Smith Eccles clear the final flight of hurdles in 1987 before winning the last of their three consecutive Champion Hurdles*

only finish seventh to Morston in the 1973 Derby.

Gelded, sold and sent to Gordon Richards for his first two seasons as a hurdler, it was after he joined Easterby that Sea Pigeon's career took off. He was beaten in his first three Champion Hurdles, but mopped up other races in that sphere and also won two Chester Cups and an Ebor Handicap on the Flat.

Sea Pigeon finally got his moment of glory in the 1980 Champion Hurdle. Jumping the final flight a length down to Monksfield, the two horses landed together and Sea Pigeon powered past his old rival to win by seven lengths.

A badly broken leg meant Jonjo O'Neill couldn't ride Sea Pigeon the following year in the Champion Hurdle, and John Francome deputised. He gave the horse, now 11, a peach of a ride to pip Pollardstown and Daring Run at the post.

Sea Pigeon retired in 1982, acclaimed one of the best dual-purpose horses racing had ever seen, and lived on to the age of 30. He and Night Nurse are buried side-by-side at Habton Grange, the Easterbys' training establishment in Yorkshire.

Heroes with Hooves

The Legend that was Arkle

Some horses are remembered for an hour, a day, a week after winning a race. Some are remembered for a lifetime – and one or two will never be forgotten. These are the horses whose achievements are so great, who work their way so deep into the hearts of racegoers, that they become immortal.

There can be no doubt as to which horse stands on the very pinnacle of the equine world's Mount Olympus. Arkle. Time and time again the question is posed, "is this horse the next Arkle?" He is the benchmark by which all others are judged.

Known to many, particularly those from his native Ireland, as "Himself", the bald facts are that he won 27 of his 35 races, including three Cheltenham Gold Cups, a King George VI Chase, two Hennessy Gold Cups and an Irish Grand National.

But those statistics don't tell you that he was a peerless steeplechaser; a brilliant jumper and effortless galloper whose performances where so superior to his contemporaries that a special handicapping system was introduced – there were one set of weights for a big race with Arkle in it, and another for a race without him.

Bred by Mary Baker and foaled at Ballymacoll Stud in Co Meath, Anne, Duchess of Westminster bought him as a three-year-old at Ballsbridge for 1,150 guineas in 1960. She named him after a

Left: *Arkle, often considered the greatest steeplechaser there's ever been, with his lad Vincent Slevis*

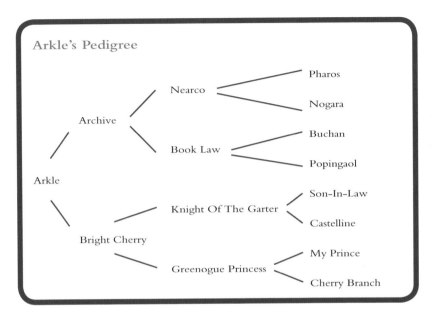

Arkle's Pedigree

mountain in Sutherland, Scotland and put him into training with Tom Dreaper.

Arkle won a couple of races over hurdles in his four-year-old season, and made his chasing debut at Cheltenham in November 1962. The 11-8 favourite won with Pat Taaffe in the saddle, and thus a legendary partnership was born.

They returned to Cheltenham for the Broadway Novices' Chase at The 1963 Festival and hacked up by 20 lengths. The

National Hunt world knew they had a bright new star on their hands – but he possibly be as good as the Fulke Walwyn-trained Mill House, who had just proved himself a hero by winning the Gold Cup?

The pair didn't meet until the Hennessy Gold Cup at Newbury that November, both having racked up more victories in the meantime in their respective countries. When Mill House gave Arkle weight and a comfortable beating in the race, it seemed to settle the matter. Good, but not quite good enough.

The 1964 Gold Cup changed that irreversibly. Despite having won three big chases in Ireland impressively in the intervening time, Arkle started at odds of 7-4 to Mill House's 8-13.

Mill House, ridden by Willie Robinson, led at a cracking pace. By the time they reached the water jump, the only other two horses in the field were struggling, while Arkle waited, going easily. He always had the bigger horse in his sights, and came upsides him at the second-last fence.

In a matter of strides he was past him. Robinson went for his whip, but it was all over. Arkle and Taaffe swept away up the hill to win effortlessly to the sound of every Irishman in the stands cheering their hearts out.

The English spectators, and Mill House's connections, were stunned. Although Mill House later put up one

more bravura performance to take the 1967 Whitbread Gold Cup, it was said that his "heart was broken" by Arkle that day.

Riding high on his own brilliance, Arkle won and won and won. A Whitbread, a Hennessy, a King George – a second Gold Cup, beating poor old Mill House by 20 lengths. He carried 2½stone more than his rivals when taking the 1964 Irish Grand National.

On it went. He made the front pages of newspapers and cinema news reels. For his third Gold Cup triumph in 1966, he started at odds of 1-10 and won by 30 lengths.

But, sadly, those who burn brightest burn out quickest and in the 1966 King George VI Chase at Kempton, he fractured a pedal bone in his hoof. He spent four months in plaster and never raced again. He was hacked out by his adoring owner and had his every whim catered for, and made celebrity appearances, including in

Did You Know...?

That Arkle's daily feed contained six eggs and two bottles of Guinness?

front of a spellbound crowd at the Horse of the Year Show, but it was a short retirement. Arkle was put down due to deteriorating health in May 1970, aged just 13.

He lives on at Cheltenham in the form of a beautiful statue by Doris Lindner, and the Arkle Bar has long been a popular – and rowdy – meeting place. The championship race for novice chasers is named after him. But even without physical representation, his ghost would haunt the course where his talent turned into greatness.

Desert Orchid: the best-loved of them all

If you ask a member of the general public to name a racehorse, the chances are that they will reply, "Desert Orchid". Nearly 25 years after the great grey retired, he is still the most famous of them all.

A flamboyant front-runner who soared over his fences, he became an icon of National Hunt racing.

Known affectionately as "Dessie", he was bred and owned by the Burridge family, who sent him into training with David Elsworth. Dessie's first race, in 1983 at Kempton over hurdles, was nearly his last – he fell heavily and took so long to get to his feet that connections thought he was dead. But he turned into a good hurdler, winning the Tolworth and Kingwell Hurdles, before going chasing in 1985.

As a novice, he won four times and finished third in the Arkle. He was seen as a two-miler, but was a surprise winner of the 1986 King George VI Chase over three miles at Kempton, starting at 16-1 and coming home victorious 15 lengths ahead of a quality field.

He continued to win over distances between two or three miles – one of his finest efforts was in the Victor Chandler Chase at Ascot over the minimum distance in 1989, where he carried 22lb more than Panto Prince and beat him by

---

Triple Winners of the Champion Hurdle

Hatton's Grace: 1949-51
Sir Ken: 1952, 1953-54
Persian War: 1968-70
See You Then: 1985-87
Istabraq: 1998-2000

a head in a thrilling finish.

Desert Orchid became more and more popular. His colour certainly helped, and his big, handsome head had a particularly distinctive look that made him instantly recognisable. But racing fans loved his bravery, his willingness and the fact that owners and trainer campaigned him widely and boldly.

He won big races under Colin Brown, Simon Sherwood and Richard Dunwoody, and the latter said: "He was this national treasure; he had such a huge following which I never experienced on any other horse so it was great, it was a big privilege to be a part of that team.

"He just had a great presence as a horse; he was grey so he stood out. He was a very intelligent horse, so as horsemen you recognise that, but he appealed to the public massively. And quite rightly so. He was the most talented horse I ever rode."

Simon Sherwood was in the plate for Dessie's most famous victory in the 1989 Cheltenham Gold Cup.

Cheltenham wasn't ever Desert Orchid's track. He had a distinct preference for right-handed courses, tending to jump to the right, especially when tired, which lost him lengths at

each fence when he was racing left-handed at Cheltenham and Aintree. And he hated deep ground.

It was a foul day, with rain, snow and sleet driving spectators indoors and turning Cheltenham's turf into a bog. All the omens were against Dessie pulling it off. But he had the heart of a lion, and overhauled the mudlark Yahoo on the run-in, spurred on by an emotional crowd screaming him on. Mud-lashed and exhausted, Dessie and Sherwood returned to scenes reminiscent of those after Arkle and Dawn Run's Gold Cups.

"I have never sat on a horse who showed such courage," said Sherwood.

Desert Orchid won 34 races in total, including four King George VI Chases, a Martell Cup, a Whitbread Gold Cup, an Irish Grand National – under top weight, by 12 lengths – a Tingle Creek and a *Racing Post* Chase.

After his retirement in 1991, he was a hugely popular sight on his many public appearances. He returned to Kempton every year to lead out the King George runners, and led the two-year-olds at Elsworth's yard in their early work for many years. He died in 2006 aged 27, and racing fans mourned him like no other horse.

Istabraq: Ireland's Champion

Just because someone isn't very good at one thing, it doesn't mean they won't excel at something else. It applies to horses, too – look at Istabraq.

Bred to win a Flat Classic, Istabraq was by multiple champion sire Sadler's Wells and a half-brother to a Derby winner in Secreto. He did win twice on the level when trained by John Gosden, but he was never to achieve the heights for which his bloodlines said he was destined.

Gosden's assistant trainer John Durkan bought him for 38,000 guineas in the summer of 1995, thinking he might make a top-flight novice hurdler and cornerstone of his own new career as a trainer in his own right. Durkan persuaded JP McManus to buy the three-year-old and Istabraq was shipped back to Ireland.

But Durkan was diagnosed with leukaemia, and Istabraq was sent to the young, up-and-coming trainer Aidan O'Brien with the understanding that Durkan would take over his training when he had recovered. Sadly Durkan never recovered and died in January 1998. But his belief in Istabraq never wavered and he listened to Istabraq's victory in the Royal & SunAlliance Novices' Hurdle at Cheltenham in March 1997 over the phone from a hospital bed in New York. He was right – and Istabraq was to become perhaps the greatest two-mile hurdler of them all.

Charlie Swan was the only jockey ever to ride Istabraq over hurdles, and together they won 23 of their 29 races. The horse was everything a hurdler should be. His lightning-quick reflexes meant he was an immaculate jumper at top speed, never wasting a fraction of a second. He had acceleration, and oozed class.

He took the Champion Hurdle in 1998, 1999 and 2000. His serious-looking, bespectacled trainer, who was only 28 when Istabraq won the first leg of his memorable treble, also sent out Theatreworld, Istabraq's galloping companion, to finished second to his stable-mate in the first two.

Istabraq seemed to fly up the Cheltenham hill to the winning post, mane streaming and nostrils flaring, in his determination to be first. If The Festival hadn't been lost to the outbreak of Foot and Mouth Disease that ravaged Britain in the spring of 2001, he would almost certainly have won a fourth Champion

Right: *Charlie Swan and Istabraq return to the winner's enclosure after their third Champion Hurdle triumph in 2000*

Hurdle, even if his powers had begun to wane by then.

There were two unexpected falls in his last few races; at the last hurdle when beaten by young pretender Moscow Flyer at Leopardstown in December 2000, and in exactly the same circumstances – although looking as though he had the race in the bag – four months later.

He was pulled up on his final appearance, in the early stages of the 2002 Champion Hurdle when never looking his old self. The Cheltenham crowd, many of who had turned up just to see the magnificent champion, applauded him as he passed the stands for the final time as hard as if he had won.

Istabraq spent a happy retirement at McManus's Martinstown Stud in Co Limerick with his best friend, Risk Of Thunder, who won seven runnings of Punchestown's La Touche Cup for his owner, film star Sean Connery.

Best Mate: Three Gold Cups

Only four horses have been awarded the honour of a statue at Cheltenham. Golden Miller, Arkle, Dawn Run – and Best Mate. The full-size Philip Blacker bronze shows just how handsome he was, with an elegant head, strong, well-formed limbs and a perfectly proportioned body. But it can't convey the talent he showed when sweeping all before him with three Gold Cup wins in 2002, 2003 and 2004. Nor can it show the affection the racing public felt for him.

He carried the claret and blue colours of owner Jim Lewis's favourite football team, Aston Villa and was trained by a consummate horsewoman, Henrietta Knight. She and her husband Terry Biddlecombe, rider of many Cheltenham winners in the 1960s and 1970s, bought him from Irish vendor Tom Costello

Did You know…?

That Sheikh Mohammed has owned two Champion Hurdle winners? The Sir Michael Stoute-trained Kribensis won for the Ruler of Dubai in 1990, and James Fanshawe trained Royal Gait to victory in 1992.

after the son of Un Desperado had won a point-to-point as a four-year-old.

His debut under Rules came at Cheltenham's November meeting in 1999, where he won the National Hunt Flat race. Best Mate was a very good hurdler, only beaten by the Noel Meade-trained Sausolito Bay in the 2000 Supreme Novices' Hurdle and winning at Aintree the following month.

But Knight and Biddlecombe knew that hurdling was only his "nursery"; he was always a steeplechaser in the making. He was a spell-binding winner of a Grade Two novices' chase at Cheltenham in November 2000 and would have been among the favourites for the Arkle the following spring if Foot and Mouth Disease hadn't intervened.

Once out of the novice ranks, he was actually beaten in open company at Ascot and Kempton, and went to his first Gold Cup in 2002 as third-favourite at 7-1 behind Looks Like Trouble, the 2000 winner, and the Nicky Henderson-trained Bacchanal. But he and Jim Culloty turned in a flawless performance. Best Mate proved he had the stamina to keep revving up the Cheltenham hill, and the ability to jump with economy and precision while in top gear.

Knight was occasionally criticised for "wrapping him up in cotton wool", and he only raced twice between then and his second Gold Cup in 2003. But would her stable star have taken the 2003 running by 10 lengths, and a returned for a third golden effort in 2004, if she had been less careful?

Comparisons are, they say, odious, and because he never ran in a handicap Best Mate didn't have the opportunity to prove he could match Arkle's weight-carrying heroics. But three Gold Cups! That's enough to place him firmly among National Hunt's all-time greats.

When he died of a heart-attack in Exeter's Haldon Gold Cup in November 2005, he made the front page of nearly every national newspaper in the country.

'King Kauto'

After Best Mate's untimely demise, the racing public thought they might have to wait years for another great chaser to come along. In fact, he was already waiting in the wings.

Kauto Star was foaled in France in 2000, and won three times over hurdles as a three-year-old and once as a four-year-old. Bloodstock agent Anthony Bromley bought him for trainer Paul Nicholls and owner Clive Smith for a reputed €400,000, and he moved to Nicholls' Somerset yard in the summer of 2004.

He made his chasing debut at Newbury on 29 December 2004, and won impressively in the skilled, sympathetic hands of Ruby Walsh. His next race ended in uproar when, in a novices' chase at Exeter, he fell at the second-last fence when 12 lengths in the

Opposite: *three-times Cheltenham Gold Cup winner Best Mate at home with his trainer, Henrietta Knight*

Knight's View

After the 2003 Gold Cup, Best Mate's trainer Henrietta Knight said: "He's not just one in a million, he's one in several million. He's the horse of a lifetime. Such an athlete with such a wonderful, effortless action."

lead. Walsh remounted, and was only beaten a short-head into second. After that, the rules were changed to forbid a horse to be remounted after it had fallen in a race.

A hock fracture kept Kauto Star out for the rest of the season and, after making his comeback at Exeter in the race in which Best Mate suffered his heart-attack, he showed just how good he was by winning the demanding, two-mile Tingle Creek Chase at Sandown. Still fairly inexperienced at the game, an ambitious plan to win the Queen Mother Champion Chase in 2006 was foiled when he fell at the third fence.

The 2006-07 season was perhaps his best. He was unbeaten in six races, proving himself a brilliant chaser who combined speed, stamina and electric jumping. As well as starting his extraordinary tally of six King George VI Chases, he demolished a good field in the Betfair Chase at Haydock by 17 lengths, and then won the Cheltenham Gold Cup in fine style from 17 other runners.

Kauto Star was fully expected to do the same a year later in 2008, but on the day he was given a fairly comprehensive beating by his stable-mate, Denman.

The two horses were so different. Kauto was quicksilver, all class and nervous tension with beautiful looks. Plainer Denman, who appealed most to the rural racegoers who saw in him National Hunt's heritage of stamina-laden, tough horses from the hunting and point-to-pointing fields, was nicknamed "The Tank". French breeding against Irish, modern against traditional – but both trained in England by one man, Paul Nicholls, and stabled in adjacent boxes at his Ditcheat yard.

The "decider", the 2009 Gold Cup, was never really that: it had been discovered in September that Denman, the strong liver-chestnut son of superb jumps sire Presenting, was suffering from a fibrillating heart. It was treated successfully and the horse ran with great credit at Cheltenham, finishing 13 lengths behind Kauto Star, but without the relentless force he had the year before. Kauto Star had become the first horse to win a Gold Cup, lose it and then win it back, and he was treated like a hero returning from war.

Neither horse won another Gold Cup. Kauto won several more races, but took a crashing fall at Cheltenham behind Imperial Commander in 2009 and pulled

up in the following year's conquest and retired. Denman took a second Hennessy in November 2009 and was runner-up to Long Run in the 2011 Gold Cup. Between them, the two horses captured the hearts of every jumps fan, and their lives after racing – Kauto Star doing dressage and giving demonstrations with the young event rider Laura Collett, and Denman hunting and team-chasing with Charlotte Alexander – are eagerly followed.

Did You know…?

That Kauto Star won 23 of his 41 races, including 16 at Grade One level?

Big Buck's: The Best Stayer in the World

The sight of a big, near-black horse with a raking stride, stalking his rivals like a menacing shadow before powering past up Cheltenham's hill will long live in the mind of anyone who saw Big Buck's win the World Hurdle. Plenty of people did – after all, he took a record four of them between 2009 and 2012.

He needed those three miles, those unforgiving undulations – and hurdles - to be seen at his all-conquering best. Bought from France by trainer Paul Nicholls and owner Andy Stewart in 2007, it was as a steeplechaser that he made his British debut that winter.

Ridden by Sam Thomas, he won by a neck from The Queen's Barbers Shop. Big Buck's obviously had class, but there were one or two niggles about his jumping. He could only finish seventh in the Jewson Novices' Handicap Chase at The Festival in 2008, five or so lengths back from winner Finger Onthe Pulse. But he won a good novices' chase at Aintree quite easily, despite making mistakes.

He made his seasonal debut later that

year in the Hennessy, but made a bad error and unshipped Sam Thomas at the last.

That was it. He returned to hurdling, and blossomed into the behemoth of the game we know. His first three

runs were all at Cheltenham and he banged in three wins, concluding with a first World Hurdle in 2009. In total, he won 18 times in succession, turning the rather overlooked division of staying hurdlers into something that

ranked alongside the Gold Cup and Champion Hurdle.

A difficult, nervy horse who was an inveterate box-walker – Ruby Walsh described him as "a bit of an oddball, but they say that about all geniuses" –

Above: *Big Buck's (left) sees off Punchestowns in 2009 to win the first of his four World Hurdles*

Opposite:
*L'Escargot, winner
of two Cheltenham
Gold Cups and a
Grand National*

he was, however, an absolutely reliable, professional racehorse.

After winning his fourth World Hurdle in March 2012, he returned from his summer holiday to win a fourth Long Distance Hurdle at Newbury in December. But shortly after that Nicholls announced that the horse, now nine, had injured a tendon and would not race again that season. He had two runs in 2013-14, but was beaten both times and was retired with full honours.

L'Escargot

Just two horses have won both the Cheltenham Gold Cup and the Grand National. Golden Miller is the only one to take both of steeplechasing's biggest prizes in the same year – 1934. But in 1975, L'Escargot took the Aintree showpiece at the fourth attempt and completed a double he had initiated with his first Gold Cup win in 1970.

L'Escargot was bred in Ireland and started his racing career there. Trainer Dan Moore first brought him to Cheltenham as a five-year-old, and he duly won division two of the Gloucestershire Hurdle – now the Supreme Novices' - under Tommy Carberry in 1968. He went chasing in 1969, and even raced a handful of times in his owner Raymond Guest's native USA, winning the prestigious Meadowbrook Chase.

His first Gold Cup triumph was something of a surprise – L'Escargot's odds were 33-1, and the favourite Kinloch Brae fell. But 1971 was a different matter; he put up a masterful display to win by 10 lengths in heavy ground.

After two Gold Cups, Guest and Moore turned their ambitions towards Aintree. L'Escargot fell at the third fence in 1972, finished third in 1973 and second in 1974 – and won in 1975, beating Red Rum by 15 lengths.

In all L'Escargot ran eight times at The Festival, also finishing second in the 1974 Cathcart Chase. He was retired to his owners' estate in Virginia, dying at the age of 21 in 1984.

The First Five Home

Festival history is full of examples of great feats of training. But one towers above the rest: the 1983 Gold Cup, where horses trained by Michael Dickinson filled the first five places.

Dickinson was 33 and in just his third season as a trainer. He had been a successful jockey, and spent two years learning from the maestro Vincent O'Brien at Ballydoyle. He had made headlines when training 12 winners on Boxing Day in 1982, including the day's big race, the King George VI Chase at Kempton.

In 1982, Silver Buck and Bregawn had won and been second in the Gold Cup, and in 1983 Dickinson brought five horses down from Yorkshire to contest the race.

Another trainer might have been said to be throwing as many darts as he could at a board in the hope that one of them connected. Not so with Dickinson, who was a meticulous planner and perfectionist with a tendency to box-walk himself; he lost a stone in the run-up to The Festival with the worry of leaving no stone unturned in his attempt to bring off a hugely ambitious plan.

Extraordinarily, he did it. Graham Bradley made all the running on Bregawn, sent off the 100-30 favourite, having decided early on in the race that the original plan, which was for Ashley House and Dermot Browne to set the pace, wasn't working. Bradley threw everything he had at Bregawn, and the brave horse responded, giving every ounce of courage and stamina to carry his jockey home in front.

Captain John and David Goulding finished second, five lengths back from Bregawn. Third was Wayward Lad (Jonjo O'Neill), probably the most talented of the five but who struggled to see out the 3¼ miles at Cheltenham. He won three King George VI Chases on Kempton's flat track, and several more of the jumping season's big chases.

Silver Buck, who had had a setback in training and missed some work, was a tired fourth under Robert Earnshaw, while Ashley House and Dermot Browne were 25 lengths behind him – but in fifth place.

It was an unprecedented achievement. Dickinson was soon "headhunted" by the major Flat owner Robert Sangster to train at the newly-renovated Manton estate in Wiltshire, and later moved to America, where he again showed majestic training skills to win two consecutive Breeders' Cup Miles with the chronically unsound Da Hoss.

Dickinson, who also developed a new kind of racing surface, Tapeta, which became popular round the world,

Above: *Michael Dickinson with the horses he trained to take the first five places in the 1983 Gold Cup*

is a regular visitor to The Festival from his home in Pennsylvania. Tanned and lean, with a shock of grey hair, he is still stopped by racegoers who want to congratulate him on his efforts of 1983.

Although Dickinson's "first five" has not yet been equalled, Paul Nicholls trained the first three home in the 2008 Gold Cup – Denman, Kauto Star and Neptune Collonges.

Michael Dickinson in Numbers

378: wins as a jockey
5: Festival winners as a jockey
3: National Hunt trainers' titles
12: winners in a day (26 December 1982)
8: Grade One winners as a trainer in the USA

The Speed Machines

Of all the races at Cheltenham, the Queen Mother Champion Chase has to be the most thrilling to watch. The sight of the brilliantly athletic two-mile chasers flying round one circuit of the track, taking their fences at lightning-speed, stirs the blood and makes the heart race.

Jockeys often say it is the most exciting race of the season to ride in. It is the ultimate test of quick reactions from horse and rider – loss of accuracy by more than a hair's breadth and you're out. There is no room for caution.

First established in 1959 as the National Hunt Two-Mile Champion Chase, it took on its present appellation in 1980 in recognition of the Queen Mother's great support and affection for jump racing.

There has been one triple winner in the race's history so far – Badsworth Boy. A spectacularly fast jumper, trained in turn by Tony, Michael and Monica Dickinson in Yorkshire, Badsworth Boy took Cheltenham by storm. His first success came in 1983 when he and Robert Earnshaw – who rode him to all his Queen Mother Champion Chase victories – beat the talented Artifice by a distance (more than 30 lengths).

His 1984 and 1985 victories were each by 10 lengths or more.

The chestnut horse with the wide white blaze wasn't quite perfect – such was his speed that he tended to get low

at his fences, and there was something of "a wing and a prayer" about his racing style. He unshipped his jockey on a couple of big occasions, but when he got it right – as he did three times at Cheltenham – he was breath-taking.

That description could also be applied to Moscow Flyer 20 years later. For the four seasons between 2001 and 2005, when he was at the height of his powers, the Jessica Harrington-trained gelding's form figures read F111F11/1U111/U111U1/111111. Either he won, or jockey Barry Geraghty ended up eating dirt.

Moscow Flyer's first visit to Cheltenham in 2002 resulted in a four-length victory over Seebald in the Arkle. He lived up to that promise in 2003, giving his rivals a seven-length drubbing in the Queen Mother Champion Chase.

But his eagerly-anticipated match against young pretender Azertyuiop and 2002 Champion Chase winner Flagship Uberalles in 2004 ended in anti-climax when he unseated Geraghty four fences from home.

The roars when he regained his crown in 2005 raised the roof of Cheltenham's grandstand. He crossed the line two lengths in front of the Martin Pipe-trained Well Chief, with Azertyuiop a further 13 lengths back.

The edge of unpredictability about Moscow Flyer added to the exhilaration of watching him race, and he became one of the sport's most-loved equine heroes.

The Queen Mother Champion Chase's record books are full of dual winners, starting with Fortria, ridden by Pat Taaffe and trained by Tom Dreaper to take the race in 1960 and 1961. Drinny's Double did indeed do the double for the famous American owner

Paul Mellon later that decade, and the 1970s sported Royal Relief, Skymas and Hilly Way as repeat champions.

After Badsworth Boy's heroics, Pearlyman, trained in Herefordshire by John Edwards, won it twice in 1987 and 1988. And David Elsworth – later to train Desert Orchid to one of the most popular Gold Cup successes of all time – managed it in the two succeeding years with Barnbrook Again.

Viking Flagship came out on top of one of the most exciting finishes of the 1990s when, in 1994, he duelled all the

Opposite:
Moscow Flyer and Barry Geraghty, Queen Mother Champion Chase winners in 2003 and 2005

Sire De Grugy and the Moore Family

National Hunt fans have soft hearts, and the 2014 Queen Mother Champion Chase winner tunnelled his way right into the centre of their affections. Sire De Grugy took the 2013-14 season by storm, winning six of his seven races and ending up as jump racing's Horse of the Year.

It was a victory for the "little guys". The chestnut with the white blaze was owned by a syndicate headed by Steve Preston, whose friends and family bought Sire De Grugy as a 50th birthday present for him. Trained by Gary Moore, for whom it was only a second Festival win, and ridden by his son Jamie – often in the shadow of his super-successful brother, Flat jockey Ryan – no winner at The Festival could have been more popular with racing fans. Even Jamie's fellow jockeys showed their appreciation, all lining the weighing-room steps to applaud his return to the winner's enclosure.

THE SPEED MACHINES

The Ryanair Chase

The Festival's newest championship race is the Ryanair Chase, run over two miles and five furlongs on the third day of the meeting. It was introduced in 2005, when The Festival grew from three days to four. It was something of an upgraded replacement of the Cathcart Challenge Cup, which had been run over the same distance, but restricted to first- and second-year chasers, for many years.

The race's registered name is The Festival Trophy, but Irish airline company Ryanair took over the sponsorship from the *Daily Telegraph* in 2006.

Albertas Run and AP McCoy doubled up in 2010 and 2011, while the Nigel Twiston-Davies-trained Imperial Commander took it in 2009, the year before his Gold Cup success.

Did You Know...?

That Cue Card, winner of the 2013 Ryanair Chase, had already tasted Festival success in the 2010 Champion Bumper? Joe Tizzard, son of Cue Card's trainer Colin, rode him on both occasions.

way up the hill with Travado and Deep Sensation. The epitome of toughness and durability, Viking Flagship ran 18 times on the Flat without winning and fell on his hurdles debut at Wolverhampton in 1990. Although the penny dropped and he won four novice hurdles in a row when trained by Martin Pipe, he only began to shine when switched to chasing (despite falling first time out again) and sent to that Colossus among Cheltenham trainers, David Nicholson.

He swerved the 1993 Arkle, but made up for it with two victories in three days at that year's Punchestown Festival, and followed up his 1994 Cheltenham

Right: *Sprinter Sacre, a dazzling winner of the 2012 Arkle Chase and the 2013 Queen Mother Champion Chase for jockey Barry Geraghty and trainer Nicky Henderson*

triumph with a more comfortable five-length win over Deep Sensation in 1995. Viking Flagship ran 73 times in his life, racking up 24 wins and a further 19 places, and carved himself deep into the racing public's affections.

Did You Know...?

That the Queen Mother, although owner of many successful horses, never managed to win the Champion Chase? The closest she came was with Game Spirit, second in 1976.

Did You Know...?

Eleven horses have, as of 2014, done the Arkle-Queen Mother Champion Chase double. The first was Fortria, and the most recent Sprinter Sacre.

Did You Know...?

That Australian-bred Crisp, most famous for being beaten into second by Red Rum in the 1973 Grand National, won the 1971 Queen Mother Champion Chase?

The most recent dual winner was Master Minded, who blew his rivals away when posting a staggering 19-length victory over Voy Por Ustedes, who had taken the race the year before, in 2008.

Trained by Paul Nicholls in Somerset but bred in France, the Clive Smith-owned Master Minded was just five years old at the time. He was odds-on to do it again in 2008, and duly obliged by seven lengths from the old warrior Well Chief.

Precocious talent does not often endure, however, and Master Minded was a disappointing fourth and then eighth in the race in 2009 and 2010, despite winning valuable races in between.

In recent years, the stand-out

performance has come from the superb Sprinter Sacre. Trained by Nicky Henderson to a facile Arkle win in 2012, he was the banker of The Festival in 2013.

At odds of 1-4, he was sent off the shortest-priced favourite at the meeting since Arkle in the 1966 Gold Cup. "Sprinter" hardly broke sweat, turning in a visually stunning display of galloping and jumping to win by 19 lengths.

His jockey was Barry Geraghty, whose record in the race of five wins – Moscow Flyer 2003 and 2005, Big Zeb in 2010, Finian's Rainbow in 2012 and then Sprinter Sacre in 2013 – is only equalled by Pat Taaffe. The latter scored on Fortria in 1960 and 1961, Ben Stack in 1964, Flyingbolt in 1966 and Straight Fort in 1970.

Flyingbolt

The outrageously talented Flyingbolt was Arkle's stable-companion and, rated only second to him in official handicap listings, would probably be as famous if they hadn't shared an era and a trainer.

Bred from a stallion (Airborne, the 1946 Derby winner) and a mare (Eastlock, by that time 19 years old) who were both supposedly barren, Flyingbolt was foaled in 1959.

He won a National Hunt Flat race on the same card as Arkle, who was two years older, at Navan in October 1963. Trainer Tom Dreaper sent both horses to Cheltenham in 1964 and, a couple of days before Arkle won his first Gold Cup, Flyingbolt took the Gloucestershire Hurdle, then the top novice race in Britain and Ireland.

He went chasing that autumn and won all five starts, including the Arkle. In the 1965-66 season he put up a remarkable effort to win the Massey Ferguson Gold Cup at Cheltenham in December, lumping 12st 6lb to victory by 15 lengths in deep ground.

At Cheltenham that spring he won the Queen Mother Champion Chase

by 15 lengths in a canter – and was only beaten three lengths the following day in the Champion Hurdle by Salmon Spray. Flyingbolt finished the season with victory in the Irish Grand National – again carrying top weight.

It looked as he might even outshine his illustrious stable-mate, but after a shocking defeat at Cheltenham in October 1966, it was discovered that he was suffering from the disease brucellosis, which he must have picked up from the cattle he had spent the summer with out at grass.

He was never the same again, and Dreaper wished him to be retired with grace. But his owners decided to keep him in training and he raced on for a couple more seasons without much success. It was a sad decline for an outstanding horse.

Jockey Barry Brogan, who rode both Arkle and Flyingbolt in their work, said many years later: "For all Arkle's brilliance, I felt Flyingbolt was the better horse. If Pat Taaffe was alive, he'd tell you the same."

Amateurs at Cheltenham

Opposite:
amateur jockey Sam Waley-Cohen (centre) after winning the the 2011 Cheltenham Gold Cup on Long Run, owned by his father Robert (behind)

The importance of the amateur rider and trainer in the history of Cheltenham cannot be overestimated. National Hunt racing's origins in the hunting and point-to-point fields have left a legacy to this day, and the sporting racegoers of modern Cheltenham appreciate and celebrate the successes of men and women who do not derive their living from the game.

Three races at The Festival are now confined to amateur riders: the Foxhunter Chase, run over the course and distance of the Gold Cup and often referred to as the amateurs' equivalent; the four-mile National Hunt Chase Challenge Cup and the three-mile, one and a half furlong Fulke Walwyn Kim Muir Challenge Cup.

The National Hunt Chase has been run more times than any other race. Although the Grand Annual is older, it was absent from Cheltenham for parts of the 19th century, while the National Hunt Chase has happened every year apart from the two World Wars, 1869, 1975 – when it was lost to waterlogging – and 2001, when Foot and Mouth Disease forced the cancellation of The Festival.

It moved around in its early years, but found a permanent home at Cheltenham in 1911.

For a long time its status was higher than that of the Gold Cup, and was only second to the Grand National in the public's affections.

Few of names of the horses who have won it are recognisable now, although Quare Times took the 1954 race the year before winning the Grand National. Topsham Bay, who won the Whitbread Gold Cup at Sandown twice, first came to prominence when victorious in the 1990 National Hunt Chase and more recently Butler's Cabin won it and the Irish Grand National in the same year, 2007.

It is running the eye down the list of winning jockeys which is more revealing. Lord Oaksey, then John Lawrence, who founded the Injured Jockeys Fund, took the 1959 renewal on Sabaria. His fellow journalist Marcus Armytage won two – in 1992 on Keep Talking and 1994 on Christmas Gorse.

Willie Mullins, who would go on to have tremendous success at Cheltenham as a trainer, pulled off a double in the saddle (Hazy Dawn, 1982 and Macks Friendly, 1984). Other Festival-winning handlers to have ridden the winner of the National Hunt Chase include Tony Martin, Philip Fenton and Mouse Morris. Ian Balding, who trained Mill Reef to win the 1971 Derby and Prix de l'Arc de Triomphe (and Crystal Spirit to win the 1991 SunAlliance Hurdle), won on Time in 1963.

JT McNamara

The perils of race-riding were brought sharply into focus at The Festival in 2013 when John Thomas "JT" McNamara, one of the most successful amateur riders of his generation, was left paralysed after a fall in the Fulke Walwyn Kim Muir Challenge Cup. McNamara had ridden four Cheltenham Festival winners: the 2002 National Hunt Chase on Rith Dubh, the first running of the Cross-Country Chase on Spot The difference in 2005, the 2007 Foxhunter on Drombeag and the 2012 National Hunt Chase on Teaforthree. Three of the four were in the famous green and gold colours of JP McManus, who was instrumental in helping fund-raise for McNamara and his family's future following the accident.

King Lucifer, and went on to ride 15 more, including two World Hurdles on My Way De Solzen in 2006 and 2007, an Arkle and a Queen Mother Champion Chase on Voy Por Ustedes and the 2008 Champion Hurdle on Katchit.

The Foxhunters is a race apart. It is a hunter chase, and therefore confined to horses which are from a hunter chase or point-to-point background, whereas the other two Festival amateur races are for horses running regularly under Rules.

Established in 1904, it is part of the fabric of The Festival. The cup awarded to the winner is famously enormous – nearly as big as the jockeys who proudly bear it aloft. Certain people – those with deep connections to the point-to-point and hunting worlds – pay more attention to it than any of the "main" races, and the paddock as the runners are led round is a glorious vision of tweed.

Some of equestrian sport's great Corinthian riders can be found among the winners. Harry Freeman-Jackson, who represented Ireland in eventing in four consecutive Olympic Games between 1952 and 1964 and won Burghley Horse Trials in 1963, rode and trained Ilolio to Foxhunter success in 1946.

The great showjumper Harry

It is the same with the Fulke Walwyn Kim Muir Challenge Cup. The odd horse, such as Nicolaus Silver, who won the Grand National weeks later in 1961, catches the eye, while Ballabriggs completed the same double across two seasons – 2010 and 2011. But while Armytage's and Oaksey's names appear again, so do those of young men who would go on to excel in the professional ranks, such as Robert Thornton. He took the 1997 race as an 18-year-old on

The Waley-Cohen family

Sam Waley-Cohen confounded expectation and rewrote the record books when, in 2011, he became the first amateur jockey for 30 years to ride the winner of the Cheltenham Gold Cup.

His first Festival victory came in 2005 aboard Liberthine in the Mildmay of Flete Handicap Chase – appropriately named after Anthony Mildmay, a leading amateur jockey who rode three Festival winners before his untimely death from drowning aged 41 in 1950.

He has also scored on Tricky Trickster in the National Hunt Chase (2009) and Rajdhani Express in the Rewards4Racing Novices' Handicap Chase (2013), but his Gold Cup victory on Long Run catapulted him to fame.

Long Run was bought by Waley-Cohen's father Robert as a four-year-old after winning eight races over hurdles and fences in France, and sent to Lambourn to be trained by Nicky Henderson. He and Sam cruised to easy victories in their first two races, including the Grade One Feltham Novices' Chase at Kempton on Boxing Day, but could only finish third behind Weapon's Amnesty and Davy Russell in the RSA Chase at The Festival in 2010.

Victory in that year's King George VI Chase meant they came to the 2011 Gold Cup as favourites to see off past winners Kauto Star, Denman – both five years older than Long Run – and Imperial Commander.

He proved a mighty victor in a strong renewal of the most prestigious chase of the season, outstaying the opposition to win by seven lengths. The reception was euphoric – Waley-Cohen was respected for holding down a full-time, demanding job as founder of the Portman Healthcare chain of dental practices, and yet his stylish, effective riding made him indistinguishable from the vastly experienced professional jockeys around him.

Horse and rider ran a creditable third in the two subsequent Gold Cups, but 2011 was their days of days.

However, the Waley-Cohen-Cheltenham love affair continues; Robert is a successful breeder of National Hunt horses at his Upton Viva Stud in Warwickshire, and more Waley-Cohen winners are almost inevitable. Robert also became chairman of the racecourse itself at the end of the 2010-2011 season. The family's combination of "amateur spirit, professional approach" sums up much of what racing fans love about Cheltenham.

Llewellyn took gold for Britain on Foxhunter at the 1952 Olympics, having won the Foxhunter on State Control four years earlier.

Several trainers' names first appeared on the Cheltenham roll of honour as Foxhunter-winning jockeys. Nick Gasalee, later to produce Party Politics to Grand National success, took the 1967 race on Mulbarton. Oliver Sherwood won on Venture To Cognac in 1984. Charlie Brooks was a popular winner with Observe in 1987, while Enda Bolger, who dominated the early runnings of the Cross-Country Chase, rode and trained Elegant Lord to victory in 1996.

Two well-known professional jockeys won the Foxhunter as teenagers – Joe Tizzard, later to be associated with dual Festival hero Cue Card, was

18 when he won with Earthmover, who famously carried Rilly Goschen to a second victory aged 13 in 2004. And Sam Twiston-Davies took the race at the same age on his father Nigel's Baby Run in 2010; three years later he was to win the Neptune Investment Management Novices' Hurdle on the top-class The New One.

Earthmover is one of a handful of horses to triumph twice in the Foxhunter. Irish-trained Salsify pulled it off in 2012 and 2013, the Richard Barber-trained Fantus won in 1995 and 1997, while Double Silk and Ron Treloggen galloped to victory in both 1993 and 1994.

Outside of the three races confined to them at The Festival, amateur winners are rare – making Sam Waley-Cohen's Gold Cup glory on Long Run in 2011 particularly special.

Did You Know...?

That Laurie Morgan, who rode and trained College Master to win the 1961 and 1962 Foxhunter, won individual and team gold medals in eventing on a horse called Salad Days at the 1960 Rome Olympics? The Australian horseman also won both Badminton Horse Trials and the Aintree Fox Hunters' on the versatile Salad Days.

Just two amateur riders have carried off the Champion Hurdle: both were Irishmen. Alan Lillingston did it in 1963 on Winning Fair, while Colin Magnier struck on For Auction in 1982.

Ted Walsh, father of Ruby and a Festival winning trainer himself and well-known pundit, is the only amateur to win the Queen Mother Champion Chase – in 1979 on Hilly Way.

Phonsie O'Brien was an amateur when he rode his brother Vincent's Cockatoo to win Division One of the Gloucestershire Hurdle, now the Supreme Novices', in 1952, and he repeated the feat in 1955 on Vindore. Bob McCreery took the Arkle aboard the George Beeby-trained Ballyatom in 1957.

Before Waley-Cohen, the last amateur to win the Gold Cup was Jim Wilson, who triumphed in 1981 aboard Little Owl. Wilson, who had upstaged the professionals the previous year by riding three winners and taking the meeting's jockeys' championships, was a marvellous all-round horseman who trained just three miles away from Prestbury Park in the village of Ham. He rode his mother-in-law Jane Pilkington's Willie Wumpkins to three Coral Golden Hurdle Final successes, and sent out Taberna Lord to win the race in 1987.

Part-owned by Wilson, Little Owl, trained by Peter Easterby in Yorkshire, beat the former Champion Hurdle winner Night Nurse and the very talented Silver Buck in 1981. In a day to remember for amateur riders, John Thorne guided Spartan Missile into fourth place in the race.

Thorne, who bred, owned and trained

LITTLE BOOK OF **CHELTENHAM**

Spartan Missile, was, like Wilson, one of the greatest amateur riders there has been. He had won one Foxhunter in 1959 on Some Baby, and added another 20 years later in 1979 with Spartan Missile.

There was tragedy in his story; Thorne had retired from race-riding to let his son Nigel take over in the late 1960s, but in 1969 Nigel was killed in a car-crash. Thorne snr returned to the saddle and won both the Cheltenham Foxhunter and the Aintree version – the latter in both 1978 and 1979 – before finishing second to Bob Champion and Aldaniti in the 1981 Grand National, aged 54.

Sadly, Thorne was killed in a point-to-pointing fall in 1982 – the year his fellow amateur Dick Saunders followed up his 1981 Cheltenham Foxhunter win with Grand National glory on Grittar.

For a while, it seemed as though Goliath had beaten David and the amateur era at Cheltenham was over. But the victories of Waley-Cohen and Nina Carberry, whose record against the professionals is unparalled amongst her sex, in recent years, have lit the flame once more.

Winning at Cheltenham: An Amateur's View

"I wasn't interested in the place to start with – for me, everything was about Aintree," says Marcus Armytage, who won the Grand National on Mr Frisk in 1990. "Then I rode my first Festival winner – Tug Of Gold in the Fulke Walwyn Kim Muir Chase in 1992 for David Nicholson.

"If it had been anywhere else apart from Cheltenham, I would have pulled the horse up, he was going so badly. But suddenly he sprouted wings and flew down the hill and up it to win.

"Suddenly, I got it. There's nothing like riding back into the winner's enclosure there – Aintree had been a bit of a blur and was all over a bit quick, whereas it takes time to ride down the hill and up into the winner's enclosure at Cheltenham. It's practically a daily occurrence for the likes of Ruby Walsh and AP McCoy, but for an amateur it is incredibly special and satisfying."

Modern Masters

Every National Hunt jockey and trainer in Britain and Ireland craves a winner at Cheltenham. Each approaches The Festival every year with desperate anticipation; for the big yards, to go home empty-handed is a disaster. For the smaller operations, a Festival winner can make a season.

Take Jim Culloty. His name may forever be enshrined in golden glory as rider of Best Mate in each of his three Cheltenham Gold Cups but, in his second career as a trainer, he had barely won a race between a first Festival victory with Lord Windermere in the RSA Chase in 2013 and the start of the 2014 meeting.

In the space of 24 hours, everything changed. Spring Heeled won the final race on Thursday afternoon, the Fulke Walwyn Kim Muir Challenge Cup and, by 3.30pm on Friday he was leading in his first Gold Cup winner as a trainer. Lord Windermere had done it again, to his trainer's amazed disbelief.

Jockey Davy Russell, himself no stranger to Festival success, described the feeling afterwards as "seventh heaven".

The man with his name on the honours board more times than any other is Nicky Henderson. By the end of the 2014 meeting he had trained an astonishing 51 Festival winners.

Henderson, who first took out a licence to train in 1978, had to wait until 1985 for his first Festival winner. But

Above: *Nicky Henderson, whose Cheltenham record is second to none, greets his winner of the 2009 Triumph Hurdle, Zaynar*

what a winner it was – See You Then in the Champion Hurdle.

Henderson tried to make a career in the City, working for stockbrokers Cazenoves, but the lure of racing was too much. He went to Fred Winter for four years to learn his trade and was also a successful amateur jockey, riding 78 winners including Sandown's Imperial Cup and the Aintree Fox Hunters'.

He trained first from Windsor House, in the centre of Lambourn, and then moved to Seven Barrows in 1992. Rarely has a Festival passed without Henderson notching up winners and his successes could easily form a book on their own. His three Champion Hurdles with the delicate See You Then proved him a master at his trade, as did his handling of the difficult, sometimes savage Remittance Man to back-to-back Queen Mother Champion Chases in

1991 and 1992.

He added a fourth Champion Hurdle with Punjabi in 2009 and a fifth with Binocular the year after.

But it wasn't until 2011 that Henderson stood on perhaps the highest podium of them all and trained a Gold Cup winner. Long Run, owned by Robert Waley-Cohen – for whom Henderson collared a World Hurdle in 1989 with Rustle, the 1999 Triumph Hurdle with Katarino and the 2005 Byrne Group Plate with Liberthine before that Gold Cup victory – gave him the full set of Cheltenham championships.

And, just to be sure, he reinforced it with a second Gold Cup courtesy of Bobs Worth in 2013.

LITTLE BOOK OF **CHELTENHAM**

Did You Know...?

That Ruby Walsh has had a song written about him? The Irish singer/songwriter Christy Moore released *The Ballad of Ruby Walsh* in 2009.

The year 2012 didn't produce a Gold Cup, but Henderson went home to Lambourn with an incredible seven winners from the meeting – the largest number by any trainer to date.

Journalist and Festival-winning jockey Marcus Armytage says: "Henderson puts all his eggs in the Cheltenham basket. He works his horses' seasons out backwards from The Festival – Cheltenham comes above everything else, almost."

The jockey who has driven in many of Henderson's recent Festival winners is Barry Geraghty, who became his stable jockey in 2008. The pair have teamed up with the likes of Bobs Worth, whose Cheltenham record includes victories in the 2011 Albert Bartlett Novices' Hurdle, the 2012 RSA Chase and the 2013 Gold Cup, and the blistering speedster Sprinter Sacre.

But Geraghty's early career at Cheltenham was closely linked to Jessica Harrington's horses. His first Festival win came aboard the magnificent Moscow Flyer in the Arkle, and Geraghty guided him to two Queen Mother Champion Chase successes after that. The smiling Irishman with the distinctive turned-down eyes was also responsible for Harrington's first Champion Hurdle victory with Jezki in 2014.

Geraghty is not the only link between Harrington and Henderson. The two families are the greatest of friends and always stay with each other for the National Hunt Festivals in their respective countries – Punchestown and Cheltenham. They may be rivals, but each will celebrate the other's success as hard as if it were their own.

Geraghty's tally of 31 Festival winners by the end of the 2014 meeting is only second to that of his countryman Ruby Walsh.

Walsh is perhaps the most stylish, natural jockey ever to grace the National Hunt riding ranks. His perfect sense of timing and uncanny understanding of how to get the best out of an individual horse marks him out in skill above possibly even the phenomenal AP McCoy.

By the age of 34 he had ridden 41 Festival winners – far more than anyone else. This is largely due to his link-ups with two of the most successful stables of the modern era, that of Paul Nicholls and Willie Mullins, but it was his outstanding talent in the saddle that got him – and

Magnificent Sevens

Ruby Walsh, 2009:

Quevega, David Nicholson Mares' Hurdle
Mikael D'Haguenet, Neptune Investment Novices' Hurdle
Cooldine, RSA Chase
Master Minded, Queen Mother Champion Chase
Big Buck's, World Hurdle
Kauto Star, Gold Cup
American Trilogy, Vincent O'Brien County Hurdle

Nicky Henderson, 2012:

Sprinter Sacre, Arkle Chase
Simonsig, Neptune Investment Management Novices' Hurdle
Bobs Worth, RSA Chase
Finian's Rainbow, Queen Mother Champion Chase
Une Artiste, Fred Winter Juvenile Handicap Hurdle
Riverside Theatre, Ryanair Chase
Bellvano, Johnny Henderson Grand Annual Chase

enabled him to keep – those jobs.

Walsh's first Festival winner was for Mullins, on Alexander Banquet in the Champion Bumper as an 18-year-old amateur. It was another four years until he secured another – the quirky Blowing Wind in the 2002 Mildmay of Flete – but that unleashed a torrent. There have been three Queen Mother Champion Chases (Azertyuiop in 2004, Master Minded 2008 and 2009); two Gold Cups, both on Kauto Star (2007 and 2009), two Champion Hurdles with Hurricane Fly in 2011 and 2013 and four World Hurdles on Big Buck's (2009-

2012). He also rode Quevega to all six of her wins in the David Nicholson Mares' Hurdle.

The son of a Festival-winning jockey and trainer – Ted Walsh, on whose Papillon Ruby scored a Grand National victory – he has been leading rider at The Festival eight times. In 2009 he rode seven winners at the meeting.

Half Walsh's Festival winners have been trained by Paul Nicholls. The son of a policeman, Nicholls never quite managed to score at the meeting in his seven-year career as a jockey, but it has been a different matter as a trainer. He started out with just a handful of horses at Manor Farm, Ditcheat in 1991, and has steadily grafted his way to the very top of the tree.

He has never made any secret of how much Festival winners mean to him, and his 34 to date have included the entire spectrum of the meeting, from the Foxhunter with Earthmover and Sleeping Night to four Gold Cups (See More Business, two with Kauto Star and one with Denman).

Nicholls's decision to return Big Buck's to the hurdling scene after a fall in the 2008 Hennessy Gold Cup at Newbury was to prove inspired, as the tall, almost black horse became the most successful horse in the history of the World Hurdle with four wins in the race.

Despite Nicholls' multiple successes with hurdlers, chasing has always his game. Until the end of The Festival in 2009, 19 of his wins at the meeting were over fences – starting with Flagship Uberalles in the 1999 Arkle – and just six were over hurdles. Curiously, in the five years after that, all nine Festival victories have been with hurdlers.

Hugely popular with the press and the public for his openness about his horses, Nicholls was lucky enough to have three of the greatest chasers of their day – Kauto Star, Denman and Master Minded in his yard at the same time.

For several years, Walsh managed to balance riding for both Nicholls and Willie Mullins – as one trains in Britain and the other Ireland, the major clashes in their calls on him only came at Cheltenham. Eventually, at the end of the 2012-2013 season, Walsh decided to concentrate his efforts at home in Ireland, where Mullins has become so dominant.

Mullins was born into racing. His father Paddy trained the only horse to win the Champion Hurdle and the Gold Cup, Dawn Run. His brothers Tom and Tony are both successful trainers, and all three were successful amateur riders.

Willie rode and trained Wither Or Which to Festival glory in the 1996 Champion Bumper, and has won that race six times in total. In 1997 British racegoers got their first sight of a horse called Florida Pearl when Mullins took the bumper with him; Florida Pearl returned the following year to win the Royal & SunAlliance Chase and became a Festival favourite, running second and third in the Gold Cup behind Looks Like Trouble and See More Business.

Three Generations of Festival Winners

Herefordshire's Scudamore family have fought on National Hunt racing's front line for six decades. Michael snr, who died in July 2014, was born into a farming and point-to-pointing family and rode the winners of the Gold Cup (Linwell, 1957) and Grand National (Oxo, 1959) during his career as a jockey.

His son Peter was champion jockey eight times, and became the first jockey to ride more than 150 winners in a season. Peter rode 13 Festival winners, chiefly for Martin Pipe, including two Champion Hurdles on Celtic Shot in 1988 and Granville Again in 1993, and the 1987 Queen Mother Champion Chase aboard Pearlyman. He now lives with his partner, trainer Lucinda Russell, in Scotland and their racing operation is going from strength to strength.

Peter's two sons, Tom and Michael jnr, have followed in the footsteps of their father and grandfather. Jockey Tom scored his first Cheltenham Festival success in 2008 aboard An Accordion in the William Hill Trophy, and has since followed it up four other victories as of 2014, chief among them Western Warhorse's 2014 Arkle win and the Ryanair Chase on Dynaste the same year.

Michael jnr is an up-and-coming trainer, whose Cheltenham triumphs include two big handicaps with Monbeg Dude in November 2012 and December 2013.

He took the leading trainer's award at The Festival for the first time in 2011, and also won it in 2013 and 2014. Hurricane Fly has given him two Champion Hurdles (2011 and 2013), and the ultra-competitive mare Quevega has been responsible for six of the 33 Festival winners he had achieved by the end of the 2014 meeting.

Mullins' influence on The Festival has not just been as rider and trainer, but also as sire of the most successful Irish amateur

rider of recent years. Patrick Mullins has scored at The Festival three times so far, all on horses trained by his father: Cousin Vinny in the 2008 Champion Bumper, Champagne Fever in the same race in 2012, and Back In Focus in the 2013 National Hunt Chase. He also provided his nephew Emmett with a first experience of the Cheltenham winner's enclosure when the 21-year-old scored with Sir Des Champs in the Martin Pipe Conditional Jockeys' Hurdle in 2011.

It is only right that Martin Pipe should have his achievements as a trainer celebrated at The Festival. He played a huge part in transforming the art of training racehorses into a science, using technology and the latest veterinary thinking in his endless quest to find an edge of his rivals.

"Winning is a drug for me," he said in an interview with the *Independent* in 1997. "I've always been competitive, in everything I do. My appetite for winning

Above: *two generations of Festival-winning trainers – David (left) and Martin Pipe*

is insatiable, and I'm never fully satisfied. That's why I carry on, year after year."

He clawed his way up the ladder, training just a single winner in his first season. It took him 14 seasons to become champion trainer, but once there he was not easily dislodged, taking the title 15 times in 17 years between 1988 and 2005. In the 1999-2000 jumps season he trained a record 243 winners.

Pipe's handling of the 1997

Champion Hurdle winner Make A Stand was typical of his never-say-die attitude to racing. Bought cheaply out of a Flat claiming race, Make A Stand had none of the good looks and physical presence expected of a superstar hurdler. But Pipe recognised much of his own toughness in the horse, and drove him up the ranks to Cheltenham glory. Make A Stand did it the hard way on 11 March 1997, making all the running and smashing the

The Champion Hurdle-Gold Cup double

Kim Bailey will never forget The Festival of 1995, by the end of which he had become only the second man to train the winners of both the Champion Hurdle and the Gold Cup in one year. Vincent O'Brien did it in 1950 with Hatton's Grace and Cottage Rake; Bailey managed it with Alderbrook and Master Oats.

Smartly-bred Alderbrook first joined Bailey as a Flat horse, and won a Group Three and a Group Two for him in that sphere before going hurdling. He was a natural, and such was Bailey's confidence in him that he contested the Champion Hurdle on just his second start. Norman Williamson rode a beautiful race on him to win by five lengths in easy style.

Alderbrook later went to stud, siring a Grade One winner in Ollie Magern.

Master Oats was a tricky horse to train; he had a tendency to bleed (break small blood vessels under stress), and had 18 months off the track with injury in the early part of his career. But he had talent, and took the Rehearsal Chase, Welsh Grand National and Cotswold Chase in the build-up to Cheltenham in the 1994–95 season. He loved the soft ground the Gold Cup was run on that year, and powered away to win by 15 lengths under Norman Williamson.

Master Oats never won again, but he gave Bailey and Williamson the second leg of the most magnificent double of them all.

course record in the process – much as his master did.

There were 34 Festival victories between Baron Blakeney's Triumph Hurdle in 1981 and Fontanesi's Vincent O'Brien County Hurdle win in 2005. They included another Champion Hurdle with Granville Again in 1993, but never a Gold Cup. Perhaps his son David, who took over at Pond House Stables in 2006 and who has already racked up 11 Festival winners, will achieve one of the very few things his father didn't.

JP McManus

The green-and-gold colours of JP McManus are the most famous in jump racing. The Irishman, a former bookmaker and a legendary gambler, is the sport's largest owner with around 400 horses in training in Britain and Ireland. Famously generous, he is an enormous contributor to charities, including many connected to racing.

His first winner at Cheltenham was Mister Donovan in the 1982 Royal & SunAlliance Novices' Hurdle, and 14 trainers have between them produced another 40 to date.

McManus's best horse was the incomparable Istabraq, who won three Champion Hurdles, but he also owned the great stayer Baracouda, two more Champion Hurdlers in Binocular and Jezki. Like-A-Butterfly and Captain Cee Bee gave him success in the Supreme Novices' Hurdle, and his other winners have been as diverse as 1996 Foxhunter hero Elegant Lord, Cross-Country Chase specialists Spot Thedifference, Garde Champetre and Heads Onthe Ground, and Albert Bartlett Novices' Hurdle victors Wichita Lineman and At Fishers Cross.

Several great jockeys were closely associated with Pipe, such as Peter Scudamore and Richard Dunwoody. But the mightiest of them all is undoubtedly AP McCoy. It is frequently said that racing will never see his like again, and it is probably true. He has broken every riding record available to him, and as of 2014 has been champion jockey 19 times in succession.

The tall, hollow-cheeked man from Moneyglass in Co Antrim rode 289 winners in the 2001-2002 season, beating Gordon Richards' tally of 269 that had stood since 1947.

His 30 Cheltenham Festival victories so far can be roughly divided into two: those he rode for Martin Pipe and, after 2004, those wearing the colours of legendary owner JP McManus. Principal

among the latter are Synchronised's 2012 Gold Cup and Binocular's 2010 Champion Hurdle.

But some of his biggest successes have come on "spare rides" – Edredon Bleu for Henrietta Knight in the 2000 Queen Mother Champion Chase, for example, while no one who saw it will forget the way he lifted the Colm Murphy-trained Brave Inca home in the 2006 Champion Hurdle.

McCoy's desperate pursuit of winners has given him a status in the public's mind greater than any other jump jockey. At Cheltenham in particular they search his face for the brief smile that flickers only when he is triumphant; on no one else's face can the desolation of failure be read more clearly. Winners are the only measure of a jockey's success, and to no one do they mean more than to McCoy, whether they come on Cheltenham's hallowed turf or in a bumper at Worcester worth only a grand to the victor.

The majority of McCoy's recent

Above: *Richard Johnson and Fingal Bay after winning the 2014 Pertemps Final*

Cheltenham winners have been trained by Jonjo O'Neill, McManus's main patron and one of Cheltenham's favourite sons.

O'Neill's twinkling smile and soft, self-deprecating humour hide a tremendous drive. His place in Cheltenham history was fixed when he rode Dawn Run to her Gold Cup triumph and Sea Pigeon to both his Champion Hurdles, but, now a "local" as his Jackdaws Castle Stables are just a few miles from the track, it is as

Richard Johnson

Although he would deny it, it is Richard Johnson's great misfortune to have been a jockey at the same time as AP McCoy. He is only second to McCoy in the number of winners he has ridden, and has finished runner-up to him in the riders' championship on many occasions.

Known as much for his politeness and the dignity with which he conducts himself as for his exceptional strength in a finish, Johnson's Cheltenham record is rosy. His long-term association with Phillip Hobbs has produced most of his 20 Festival winners to date, including a Champion Hurdle in 2003 on Rooster Booster , Triumph Hurdles on Made In Japan (2004) and Detroit City (2006), an Arkle on Captain Chris in 2011 and a Supreme Novices' with Menorah in 2010. Their first success together was the 2002 Queen Mother Champion Chase with Flagship Uberalles.

But his remaining pair of victories in The Festival's championships came from other sources. His first boss David Nicholson trained Stayers' Hurdle winner Anzum. And Noel Chance – later to become Johnson's father-in-law when he married Chance's daughter Fiona – had charge of Gold Cup hero Looks Like Trouble.

a trainer that he is best known.

In his first 15 years as a trainer he scored just three times at The Festival. But his move to Gloucestershire in 2001 turned on the tap, and by the conclusion of the 2014 Festival he had trained a further 23 winners at the meeting – and many more on days outside The Festival.

Iris's Gift gave his first success in a championship race when the grey took the 2004 World Hurdle, and in 2014 More Of That took the same contest. Albertas Run put O'Neill's name on the Ryanair Chase trophy in 2010 and 2011 and when Synchronised won the 2012 Gold Cup, he became the second man to both ride and train a winner of the race after Fred Winter.

The French Invasion

Cheltenham is always envisaged as a battleground between two sides: the Irish and the British. But occasionally a third combatant sneaks in and carries off the prizes.

Many Cheltenham winners have been bred in France – Kauto Star, Master Minded and Long Run all grew up on the other side of the Channel, for example. But a select few have been trained there.

It starts, surprisingly, as far back as 1956, when the Anglo-French trainer Harry Count brought Tasmin over to win the second division of the Gloucestershire Hurdle.

But the most prolific visitor has been Francois Doumen. Equally as successful on the Flat with horses such as Jim And Tonic as he has been over jumps, Doumen started targeting the Cheltenham Gold Cup in the early 1990s with The Fellow. In 1991 he finished second to Garrison Savannah; in 1992 he was runner-up to Cool Ground. Jodami beat him into fourth in 1993, but he gave it one more shot in 1994 – and won.

Doumen charmed British racing fans with his perfect English and his urbane sense of humour, and they gallantly applauded his Triumph Hurdle victory with Snowdrop in 2000. It was the warhorse Baracouda who they took to their hearts, however; after three wins at the Parisian track Auteuil in 2000,

Sir Peter and the Marquesa

The Marquesa de Moratella, owner of 1994 Gold Cup winner The Fellow, also owned dual Stayers' Hurdle hero Baracouda and King George VI Chase winner First Gold until she sold them to Irish owner JP McManus late 2000. The deal was brokered by the Marquesa's good friend and adviser Sir Peter O'Sullevan, long-term BBC commentator and the "voice of racing".

He first met the Marquesa through her brother, the sporting Spanish amateur jockey the Marquis de Portago, who rode Garde Toi into third place behind Cottage Rake in the 1950 Gold Cup.

Sir Peter enjoyed the unique distinction of commentating on the victory of his own horse at The Festival in 1974 when Attivo won the Triumph Hurdle.

As the horse crossed the line, the ever-professional Sir Peter uttered, "And it's first Attivo, owned by, uh, Peter O'Sullevan…"

14 of the remaining 15 successes of his impressive career came at English tracks.

The greatest of these were, of course, his Stayers' Hurdle triumphs in 2002 and 2003. He was ridden on both occasions by Doumen's son Thierry, who himself trained – and rode – Foreman to be placed twice at The Festival.

Wily Baracouda was a "hold-up horse", who usually required his jockey to be patient and deliver him with a late burst to catch his rivals in the shadow of the winning post. The only exception to this was at Ascot, when his three Long Walk Hurdle successes came with winning distances of 14 lengths, 24 lengths and 30 lengths.

Baracouda spent his retirement at his owner JP McManus's stud in Ireland, sharing a field with his fellow Frenchman First Gold, winner of big races at Aintree and Punchestown.

THE FRENCH INVASION

Right: *Thierry Doumen and Baracouda (left), dual winners of the World Hurdle for owner JP McManus and trainer Francois Doumen*

Before Francois Doumen decided to concentrate his energies solely on the Flat in 2010, he trained two more Festival winners, both in 2005 and both ridden by Robert Thornton: Moulin Riche in the Brit Insurance Novices' Hurdle and Kelami in the William Hill Chase.

He also brought over Kasbah Bliss, later to win a Group One on the Flat, to finish second to Inglis Drever in the 2008 World Hurdle.

The most successful French jumps trainer of recent times is the Pau-based Guillame Macaire, and he has made sporadic raids on Cheltenham. The closest he has come to Festival triumph was with Jair Du Cochet, who won a Grade Two hurdle at Cheltenham in January 2001, finished second to One Knight in the 2003 Royal & SunAlliance Chase and took the Pillar Property Chase in 2004. The latter success made him second favourite for the Gold Cup behind Best Mate – but tragedy struck and Jair Du Cochet broke a leg on the gallops a week before the race.

French runners have sadly been few and far between in recent years. When will the tricolore be hoisted high at Cheltenham again?

Women at Cheltenham

Training Pioneers

Racing has always been a sport largely dominated by men. Women were not permitted to hold training licences until Florence Nagle took The Jockey Club to court over the issue in 1966, although there had been several cases of women doing the hard work of training winners while a man nominally held the licence.

And although female jockeys had been prolific in the amateur point-to-point field for decades, they were banned from riding under Rules in Britain until 1972.

In 1970, Delma Harty laid the foundation stone for female achievements at Cheltenham when training Khan –

owned and ridden by Lord Petersham – to win the County Hurdle at The Festival.

Over the subsequent decade, a trickle of determined women made their mark. In 1972 Katie Gaze became the first to train a double at The Festival when Even Dawn won the Aldsworth Hurdle and Cold Day took the County Hurdle. Gaze trained at her family's Caradoc Court in Herefordshire – later the source of several more Festival winners when John Edwards produced the likes of dual Queen Mother Champion Chase hero Pearlyman from its picturesque slopes.

Barbara Surman won the Christie's Foxhunter with Real Rascal in 1975; Caroline Mason trained Waggoners Walk to victory in the 1980 National Hunt

Chase and the 1981 Kim Muir Chase. Dina Smith coaxed Shiny Copper to Triumph Hurdle glory at 66-1 in 1982. And Jane Pilkington made her mark on racing history when she produced Willie Wumpkins to win three consecutive Coral Golden Hurdles between 1979 and 1981.

But it took until 1983 for a woman to train the winner of a championship race at The Festival. The horse was Gaye Brief, the race was the Champion Hurdle and the trainer was Mercy Rimell.

Famously uncompromising and racing's "iron lady", Rimell dressed immaculately and did not suffer fools gladly. She took over the training licence at Kinnersley, after her husband Fred, one of the greatest National Hunt trainers of the 20th century, died suddenly in 1981. The year after Gaye Brief's Champion Hurdle, the horse's full-brother, Gaye Chance, won the Stayers' Hurdle – and in 1987 Gala's Image added another big race to Rimell's record when taking the Arkle Chase.

A month after Gaye Brief's Champion Hurdle, another formidable female made an indelible mark on the racing

Dorothy Paget

Many women have owned winners at Cheltenham. But there will never be another like the Hon Dorothy Paget, the fabulously wealthy eccentric whose horses racked her up an impressive 68 winners at the track between 1932 and 1957.

The most famous of her stable was the incomparable Golden Miller, winner of five Gold Cups – and a Grand National. Roman Hackle (1940) and Mont Tremblant (1952) gave her a further two Gold Cups, while her four Champion Hurdle triumphs were delivered by Insurance in 1932 and 1933, Solford in 1940 and Distel in 1946.

Paget owned Ballymacoll Stud in Co Meath, and it was there that Arkle was foaled in 1957. She was leading National Hunt owner six times, and champion owner on the Flat in 1943 – the year her homebred Straight Deal won the Derby. She also owned showjumpers, ridden by Peggy "Pug" Whitehead – grandmother of Cheltenham-winning jockey Gee Armytage.

Her quixotic temperament meant that she changed trainers frequently. She bet huge sums of money on racing – mainly at night, over the telephone, on races that had already taken place. Her bookmakers entirely trusted her oath that she did not already know the result. When driving to the races, she insisted that a second Rolls-Royce followed her in case the one she was in broke down.

Paget died aged just 54 in 1960.

world by becoming the first woman to train the winner of the Grand National. Jenny Pitman made headlines round the world when Corbière took the Aintree spectacle and, proving it was no fluke, she conquered yet another bastion the following year in 1984. This time she won the Cheltenham Gold Cup with Burrough Hill Lad.

The eight-year-old bay had established

himself as a leading contender for the Gold Cup when winning the Welsh National at Chepstow the previous December and, ridden by Phil Tuck, took the Cheltenham highlight by three lengths at odds of 7-2. Once of the best chasers of his generation, his other glories included the 1984 Hennessy Gold Cup at Newbury under top weight and that season's King George VI Chase at Kempton. He lived until the age of 28, dying in January 2004.

The full set of championship races won by women was completed in 1985, when Monica Dickinson took the Queen Mother Champion Chase with Badsworth Boy, who had won the previous two runnings of the race when trained by her son Michael.

The Dickinson family trained at Harewood in Yorkshire. Monica had been British ladies' showjumping champion in 1950, just a few months after giving birth Michael, who went on to take his place in the Cheltenham record books when he trained the first five horses home in the 1983 Gold Cup.

Badsworth Boy was Dickinson's only Festival winner, but she came close to taking the Gold Cup the same year when Righthand Man was second to Forgive

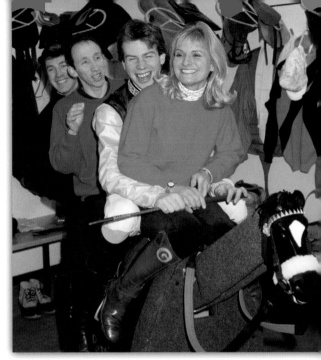

Above: *Gee Armytage (right) was a successful professional jockey and rode a double at The Festival in 1987*

'N Forget.

Burrough Hill Lad was the first Festival winner Pitman trained from her Lambourn yard, but several more were to follow. A second Gold Cup triumph was to follow in 1991 with Garrison Savannah, ridden by her son Mark. A month later Garrison Savannah and Mark finished a brave second in the Grand National, only being overtaken in the last two furlongs by Seagram.

Pitman also achieved a Supreme Novices' Hurdle victory with Indefence in 1996, the 1987 running of the National Hunt Handicap Chase with Gainsay, SunAlliance Chases with Garrison Savannah in 1990 and Nahthen Lad in 1996 and the Stayers' Hurdle in 1998 with Princeful.

Jenny Pitman was the first really successful professional female trainer. She started out working in racing as a stable-girl in her teens, and began training point-to-pointers in 1975, taking out a full licence the following year. Awarded an OBE for services to racing in 1998, she retired from training in 1999.

The year before Pitman's final Festival winner in 1998, Henrietta Knight's name was first inscribed in Cheltenham's annals. Owned by Lord Vestey, Cheltenham's chairman from 1990-2011 and married to Knight's sister Celia, Karshi was a surprise winner of the Stayers' Hurdle under Jamie Osborne, starting at 20-1.

In 1998 Knight, who taught biology and history before taking out a training licence, won the Grand Annual Chase with Edredon Bleu. The little French-bred gelding, whose name translates as "Blue Eiderdown", was a very popular winner of the Queen Mother Champion Chase two

years later in 2000 under AP McCoy.

That millennium year Knight also won the SunAlliance Chase with Lord Noelie. The jockey on that occasion was Jim Culloty, and the Irishman was in the saddle for the three victories that transformed Knight into a Cheltenham legend. They were, of course, courtesy of Best Mate, who thrilled the Prestbury crowds by taking the Gold Cup in 2002, 2003 and 2004.

Knight came from an eventing background, finishing 12th at Badminton Horse Trials in 1973, and chaired the selection committee for the British team from 1984-1988. During that period she trained more than 100 point-to-point winners from her Wantage yard, and in 1989 took out a full licence.

In 1995 she married Terry Biddlecombe, former champion National Hunt jockey and winner of the 1967 Gold Cup on Woodland Venture.

As "Hen and Terry", the pair became part of Cheltenham mythology. Knight could never bear to watch her horses run in the big races and, always wearing the same lucky blue suit and string of pearls, hid herself from view. When "Matey", as Best Mate was nicknamed by Knight, galloped to victory up the Cheltenham

hill for a third time, Knight's own televised gallop down to the course to meet him, flinging herself into Biddlecombe's arms, became one of the most evocative Cheltenham memories of a generation. Biddlecombe's emotions always got the better of him and his ruddy cheeks would stream with tears after a victory.

Soon after Knight trained her first Festival winner, another leading lady got off the mark for the first time. By the end of The Festival in 2014, Jessica Harrington had seen her horses flash past the winning post in first place eight times.

Harrington is another whose roots are in the sport of eventing; she represented Ireland in three European Championships, one world championship and the 1980 Alternative Olympics (many nations boycotted the Moscow Olympics that year and a substitute competition

Did You Know…?

That Dubacilla only ran three times at Cheltenham, winning the Cotswold Chase in January 1994, finishing second in the following year's race – and was also second to Master Oats in the 1995 Gold Cup? The David Nicholson-trained mare was also the dam of four winners.

Did You Know…?

That three sets of brothers and sisters have ridden Cheltenham winners: Marcus and Gee Armytage, Nina, Philip and Paul Carberry and Ruby and Katie Walsh?

was held at Fontainebleau in France). She took over her husband Johnny's training permit in the late 1980s, and upgraded to a full licence a few years later.

Her success at Cheltenham started in 1999 with Space Trucker, who took the Grand Annual Chase. Then came the great Moscow Flyer, the brilliantly fast two-mile chaser who won the Arkle in 2002 and then the Queen Mother Champion Chase in 2003 and 2005.

Spirit Leader took the 2003 County Hurdle for Harrington's Commonstown Stables in Co Kildare, and Cork All Star (2007 Champion Bumper) and Bostons Angel (2011 RSA Chase) also struck.

These victories were topped in 2014 when Jezki powered home under Barry Geraghty – who had ridden Moscow Flyer to his three Cheltenham triumphs – to win the Champion Hurdle by a neck. Harrington was the first woman to train a Champion Hurdle winner since Mercy Rimell 31 years earlier.

In the present era, more and more women are adding their names to The Festival score sheet. Emma Lavelle has knocked in two victories, in 2008 with Crack Away Jack in the Fred Winter Juvenile Hurdle and Pause And Clause in the Martin Pipe Conditional Jockeys' Hurdle. Venetia Williams has a tally of

Opposite:
Festival-winning trainer Venetia Williams

six; Sue Smith and Lucinda Russell have one apiece. Rebecca Curtis, who trains in West Wales, has had an excellent start to her training career with a winner in 2012 (Teaforthree in the National Hunt Chase), one in 2013 (At Fishers Cross, Albert Bartlett Novices' Hurdle) and another in 2014 (O'Faolains Boy, RSA Chase). They will all undoubtedly add to those in the years to come.

In the Saddle

Caroline Beasley was the first woman to ride a Festival winner at Cheltenham, taking the 1983 Foxhunter on the Irish-trained Eliogarty. Before her, Caroline Saunders – now a successful trainer under her married name of Bailey – became the first lady to win a race at Cheltenham in May 1978, when she won the Vale of Evesham Hunter Chase on Ptarmigan III.

Since then, four more women have won "the amateurs' Gold Cup" – Katie Rimell in 1989 on Three Counties, trained by her grandmother Mercy; Polly Curling, on Fantus in 1995; Fiona Needham in 2002 on Last Option, and Rilly Goschen, who rode Earthmover for Paul Nicholls in 2004.

But the handful of women to have scored against professional jockeys is even smaller. Gee Armytage led the way when she won the Mildmay of Flete Handicap Chase in 1987 on Gee-A. She was just 22, and earlier in the week she had already taken the Kim Muir on The Ellier. It was an enormous achievement for a woman just to get a ride at The Festival, let alone win two races. Armytage actually tied with Peter Scudamore for the meeting's leading jockey title with two wins from five rides, but lost out because Scudamore had ridden more horses to be placed.

It seemed as though the floodgates might have been opened, but in actual fact the 1980s were to prove the glory days of female National Hunt jockeys, with several – including Armytage – turning professional. Lorna Vincent won three races at Cheltenham meetings outside of The Festival. A spate of terrible falls halted their trajectory, and it wasn't until the appearance of two Irish girls, born into families steeped in racing, two decades later that women featured outside the Foxhunter again.

In 2005 Nina Carberry, then 20, brought Dabiroun home to win the Fred Winter Juvenile Novices' Hurdle to a storm of publicity. Since then she has ridden a further three winners, all in the Cross-Country Chase: Heads Ontheground in 2007, and Garde Champetre in 2008 and 2009.

Carberry is the daughter of Gold Cup-winning rider and later trainer Tommy and sister of jockey Paul, whose Festival count stands at 14 as of 2014. She was born to ride, and is possibly the strongest, most stylish female yet to light up a racecourse. She also has an Irish Grand National to her credit, taking the famous handicap in 2011.

In 2010, Carberry and her great friend Katie Walsh – later to become her sister-in-law when Carberry married Walsh's brother Ted in 2012 – fought a tremendous battle in the closing stages of the National Hunt Chase. Walsh prevailed on Poker De Sivola, with Carberry second on Becauseicouldntsee.

Walsh, daughter of trainer Ted and sister of Cheltenham's winning-most jockey Ruby, joined that illustrious group of female jockeys to have won races against professionals later on in that 2010 meeting when she won the County Hurdle on Thousand Stars. It is a group with just three members – who will be the next to force her way into its ranks?

Great Mares

Quevega truly deserves to be called "Queen of Cheltenham." In 2014, the diminutive bay mare became the first horse in history to win at six consecutive Festivals, overtaking Golden Miller's long-time record.

Trained in Co Carlow, Ireland by Willie Mullins and ridden in all six of her Cheltenham races by Ruby Walsh, Quevega won the David Nicholson Mares' Hurdle every year from 2009-2014. The Cheltenham crowd grew to adore her, and the reception she received as she strode back into the winner's enclosure, ears pricked, grew more and more joyous with every passing year.

Foaled in 2004, Quevega started her career in France, winning three National Hunt Flat races before transferring to Mullins' care in Ireland. He campaigned her with great care, and she won 13 of her 18 races for him – including four World Series Hurdles at the Punchestown Festival - before retiring to stud in 2014.

Mullins said after her sixth victory: "She's got stamina, speed and everything. She's just class – what more can I say? I'm so pleased for her and she has her own place in history now. Just to get a horse here for six years in a row is enough."

The David Nicholson Mares' Hurdle was established in 2008 – the Donald McCain jnr-trained Whiteoak won the first running – as part of an initiative to provide more racing opportunities for National Hunt mares in Britain, and therefore to encourage owners and trainers to purchase more mares at the bloodstock sales and to make greater efforts to keep them in training. It has become an instant hit, due to the superstar who has won six of its seven renewals, and has recently been elevated to Grade One status.

No other mare can begin to live up to Quevega's strike-rate at Cheltenham, but even she takes second place to Dawn Run in the public's affection.

Dawn Run, whose statue looks proudly down on the Cheltenham parade ring, remains the only horse to win both the Champion Hurdle and the Gold Cup. Her story in an exceptionally romantic one, and Sir Peter O'Sullevan's commentary on her Gold Cup triumph, "and the mare's beginning to get up…" makes listeners' ears prick with tears of emotion.

Owned by Charmian Hill, who rode

her in her first three races, Dawn Run was trained in Ireland by Paddy Mullins. She was champion novice hurdler in her first season, 1982-83, and became the first horse to win the Champion Hurdle at Cheltenham, the Irish Champion Hurdle at Leopardstown and the French Champion Hurdle at Auteuil the following season.

A big, strapping bay mare with a plain head and a pugnacious attitude, Dawn Run was having only her fifth start over fences when she ran in the 1986 Gold Cup. Although Mullins' son Tony had ridden her up to that point, he was controversially replaced by Jonjo O'Neill for Cheltenham after falling off her on her previous start.

Dawn Run and O'Neill led the field round the final turn at the bottom of the

Records of Female Trainers at The Festival up to 2014

Jessica Harrington: 8 winners
Jenny Pitman: 7 winners
Henrietta Knight: 6 winners
Venetia Williams: 6 winners
Mercy Rimell: 4 winners

hill, but three-times King George VI Chase winner Wayward Lad and the 1985 Gold Cup winner Forgive 'N Forget swept past her. But the indefatigable mare battled on, and just caught Wayward Lad a few yards from the line.

The reception was deafening and the crowd surged into the winner's enclosure as the pair returned, swamping horse, jockey and trainer in their wild celebrations.

"I had job hanging on to my weights and my saddle trying to get back in to get weighed," said O'Neill years later. "They were grabbing hairs from her tail."

Tragically, Dawn Run was killed in the French Champion Hurdle later that season, breaking her neck when falling at the fifth-last. An Irish ballad was written about her, and she has passed into racing immortality.

Only two other mares have, as of 2014, won the Champion Hurdle. The first was African Sister, ridden by Keith Piggott, father of legendary Flat jockey Lester, on the eve of the Second World War in 1939. And Flakey Dove, bred, owned and trained by the Price family from Herefordshire, who took the 1994 renewal.

And only three mares have matched Dawn Run's Gold Cup victory. Ballinod, trained by Frank Morgan in Ireland won the race in 1925; the Verly Bewicke-trained Kerstin did it in 1958 and Francis Flood handled Glencaraig Lady to her 1972 triumph.

The World Hurdle has only gone to mares twice in its history – Rose Ravine,

trained by Fulke Walwyn, in 1985, and the Paddy Kiely-trained Shuil Ar Aghaidh in 1993.

The most recent filly to win the Triumph Hurdle was the French-trained Snowdrop in 2000, while the highly talented Like-A-Butterfly took the 2002 Supreme Novices' Hurdle – a race also won by French Ballerina four years earlier. To find an Arkle Chase-winning mare, you have to look back to Anaglog's Daughter, trained by Tommy Carberry, in 1980.

But Cheltenham isn't only about The Festival, and one of the most popular hurdling mares of recent times claimed Cheltenham as her own. Lady Rebecca, trained by Venetia Williams, cost only 400 guineas at auction, but won 13 of her 19 races, including the Cleeve Hurdle in 1999, 2000 and 2001.

Lady Cricket took the 2000 Paddy Power Gold Cup – and one of her offspring, Red Sherlock, won a Grade Two hurdle at Cheltenham in January 2014.

Beyond The Festival

The four days of The Festival may be the axis on which the world of National Hunt racing turns, but the racecourse doesn't lie in patient hibernation for the other 361 days of the year.

The jump racing season at Prestbury Park commences in October with the two-day Showcase meeting. This is often spectators' first opportunity to see the horses who will soar to stardom over the next few months. The feature race is the Showcase Trophy, won in 2011 and 2013 by the Phillip Hobbs-trained Cheltenham specialist Balthazar King, who is a dual winner of the Cross-Country Chase at The Festival in March.

The highlight of November for any National Hunt fan is Cheltenham's three-day Open meeting. It starts with Countryside Day, during which the sport celebrates its roots in and links to the hunting and equestrian communities. The feature race is, appropriately enough, the Cross-Country Chase over the specially-designed track in the centre of the course.

The middle day of the meeting is Paddy Power Gold Cup day. Inaugurated in 1960, this 2½-mile handicap chase was sponsored by Mackeson for the first 35 years of its existence. Murphy's and Thomas Pink took their turn, and Irish bookmakers Paddy Power have given it their name since 2003.

Its roll of honour is straight from National Hunt's "A" list; the two of the first three runnings went to Fortria, the exceptionally versatile son of Gold Cup winner Fortina trained by Tom Dreaper and ridden by Pat Taaffe. Fortria won two Champion Chases over two miles, an Irish Grand National over 3½ miles and was only beaten a length in a Gold Cup.

Gay Trip sandwiched a Grand National victory in 1970 between two Mackeson Gold Cups in 1969 and 1971, while Imperial Commander took the Paddy Power two seasons before his Cheltenham Gold Cup triumph.

The Somerset trainer Martin Pipe's name was inextricably linked with the race. Beau Ranger Bay gave him his first success in 1987, then between 1996 (Challenger Du Luc) and 2005 (Our Vic) he won it seven times.

Finally, the meeting concludes with Cheltenham's only Sunday raceday of the season – The Open Sunday – starring the Greatwood Hurdle, a highly competitive handicap that attracts the big names in that division.

December's two-day meeting includes another Cross-Country Chase, the Relkeel Hurdle and the International Hurdle (formerly known as the Bula Hurdle).

The New Year's Day meeting has

become a very popular way to clear the cobwebs away from the celebrations of the night before. Its feature race is the Dipper Novices' Chase, and in 2007 My Way De Solzen – the previous year's World Hurdle winner – took en route to Arkle victory at The Festival.

There is a second meeting in January – Festival Trials Day. As the name suggests, it is used by many trainers as a preparation for The Festival six or seven weeks later.

It is a day of top-class racing, but two races in particular have distinguished histories.

Above: *Lady Rebecca and Norman Williamson after the third of their Cleeve Hurdle successes*

Above: *Imperial Commander, who later took the 2010 Gold Cup, scores a 16-length win at Cheltenham's Showcase meeting in October 2007*

The Cleeve Hurdle, effectively a trial for the World Hurdle at The Festival but a significant target in its own right, has been won by all the best staying hurdlers in the past couple of decades. For more than a decade a Grade One race, it was downgraded to Grade Two status in 2004.

The Venetia Williams-trained Lady Rebecca made the race her own, winning it in 1999, 2000 and 2001.

Both the great champions Inglis Drever and Big Buck's have notched up wins in it; Inglis Drever in 2008 and Big Buck's in 2009 and 2012.

And the Grade Two Cotswold

The International Hurdle

The International Hurdle, run at the December meeting, was previously called the Bula Hurdle. Two horses have won it three times – Bird's Nest and Relkeel.

Bird's Nest was trained by Bob Turnell and ridden by his son Andy. He won the Bula in 1977, 1978 and 1980, and also took a Christmas Hurdle at Kempton and two Scottish Champion Hurdles, as well as finishing second to Night Nurse in the 1976 Champion Hurdle at The Festival.

Relkeel, trained first by David Nicholson and then Alan King, took it in 1997, 1998 and 1999. Richard Johnson rode him in his first and third successes, while Adrian Maguire was on board in 1998. A Grade Two race named after the horse is also run at the December meeting.

Chase – the registered name of the race currently known for sponsorship reasons as the Argento Chase - serves as a Gold Cup trial on the same card. The Paul Nicholls-trained See More Business is one of several horses to have completed the double; he won the race in 1999, just weeks before his Gold Cup triumph, and again in 2001.

Master Oats (1995) and Looks Like Trouble (2000) also had successful dry-runs for their Gold Cup heroics.

After the headlong madness of The Festival, racegoers have a month to rinse out their livers and refill their wallets before returning to Prestbury Park for the two-day April meeting, at which many horses who came up just slightly short in the white heat of The Festival come to claim compensation.

The season concludes with the laid-back, friendly vibe of the Hunter Chase Evening. The racing is still highly competitive, with the best hunter chasers and point-to-pointers vying for championship crowns, but the atmosphere is less intense as spring rolls into summer.

Martin Pipe's Eight Paddy Power Gold Cup Winners

1987: Beau Ranger
1996: Challenger Du Luc
1998: Cyfor Malta
2000: Lady Cricket
2001: Shooting Light
2002: Cyfor Malta
2004: Celestial Gold
2005: Our Vic

Behind the Scenes

Cheltenham Racecourse could be envisaged as a swan, sliding swiftly and serenely through the water. Beneath the surface, however, there is a less tranquil scene as the "legs" work ceaselessly and energetically to power the swan forward.

The core of about 60 permanent staff swells to 4,500 employed during The Festival, when 235,000 spectators flood in through the gates over the four days of racing.

Improvement has always been at the fore-front of those who have run the racecourse's minds.

In 1960 a second new stand was provided in the Tattersalls' enclosure and the Members' Lawn extended, while the main grandstand was extended twice in the 1980s. In 1982 the parade ring, winner's enclosure and weighing-room was rebuilt behind the stands, and in 1987 further changes were made to the Tattersalls' enclosure.

The Best Mate enclosure, between the top bend of the track and the stables, was added in 2003-2004, and the vast Centaur hall in the main grandstand building added.

The course itself has developed considerably over the decades and there are now three tracks: the Old course, used for October, November and the first two days of The Festival each year; the New course, introduced in 1965 and raced on in December, January, the third

The Courses

Anyone with a real interest in jump racing should take the trouble to walk the track at Cheltenham. Only then can one appreciate its undulations – such as the remains of ancient ridge-and-furrow down the back straight, and just how much of a rollercoaster it is running down the hill, round the final bend and up the stiff final climb to the winning post. It is a tough, challenging track that perfectly tests a National Hunt horse's essential attributes of jumping skill, stamina and speed.

The Old and New courses run alongside each other, left-handed. The Old course is about a mile and a half with nine fences, while the New course is just slightly longer and has 10 fences on it.

The Cross-Country course is contained in the middle of the track, jumping just the final fence on the "racecourse proper". Thirty-two obstacles are jumped during a Cross-Country race, and they range from hedges to rails, banks and stuffed hurdles.

Simon Claisse has been the popular and highly respected clerk of the course at Cheltenham since 2000.

and fourth days of The Festival and in April and May, and the Cross-Country course, used only for the three races over its specialist obstacles throughout the season.

In March 2013, Cheltenham's owners, Jockey Club Racecourses, announced plans for a £45million redevelopment of the course's facilities. At the heart of this was a new, state-of-the-art main grandstand with a capacity of 6,500 to replace the one built in the 1920s.

The redevelopment has taken place in careful stages, with the first real change noticed by racegoers being the replacement of the old "A&R" private boxes with a smart temporary structure for the 2013-14 season.

Most of the work took place in the summer of 2014, ahead of the new

Bloodstock Sales at Cheltenham

There are four auctions of National Hunt horses at Cheltenham in the 2014-15 season, run by the Brightwells, which first started holding sales at the track in 2004.

2014-15 season, but work will continue over the winter in between racedays. The redevelopment, which includes considerable work on facilities such as bars and loos, as well as a new Royal Box and other hospitality areas, and better viewing of the course and parade ring, should be completed for The Festival 2016.

This is Jockey Club Racecourses' biggest-ever single investment project. How appropriate that the organisation has chosen Cheltenham – for neither would exist without the other.

In 1964, worries over possible loss of the site for urban development led to the formation of the Racecourse Holdings Trust. A consortium, led by Johnny Henderson, father of top trainer Nicky, put their heads together and bought Prestbury Park for £240,000. Johnny Henderson was a highly successful stockbroker and a hunting and racing man, and his initiative led to what is now

called Jockey Club Racecourses – 15 tracks that include Aintree, Epsom and the two Newmarket courses. It is the country's premier racecourse group – and Cheltenham is the most profitable of the bunch. The Jockey Club acts for the good of British racing, and all profits are put back into the sport.

In 2005 Johnny Henderson's name was added to The Festival's oldest race, the Grand Annual Chase, in recognition in the part he played in building Cheltenham's future. His son Nicky

Who Sculpted Cheltenham's Statues?

Golden Miller: Judy Boyt
Arkle: Doris Lindner
Best Mate: Philip Blacker
Dawn Run: Jonathan Knight
The Queen Mother: Angela Conner

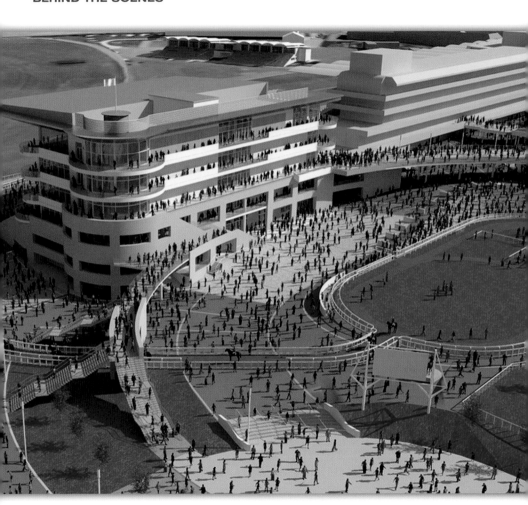

trained the winner in 2006 (Greenhope) and 2012 (Bellvano).

As the racecourse has expanded, so have its interests. As well as 16 days' racing a year, the site is host to myriad other events. Comedians, bands and circuses perform within its confines, and Christmas parties, balls, awards ceremonies and conferences, large or small, are held there.

The Centaur, Cheltenham Racecourse's largest facility, can be used as a theatre, to hold a dinner-dance for more than 1,000 people – and even as a bloodstock auction venue.

In 2012 Ian Renton took over the reins as director from Edward Gillespie, who had spent 32 years at the helm. Renton, who also has responsibility for Exeter, Warwick and Wincanton under his official title of south-west regional director of Jockey Club Racecourses, was assistant manager at Cheltenham in the 1980s.

Opposite: *the new grandstand*

Did You Know...?

That at the 2013 Festival, 236,472 pints of Guinness were drunk?

Did You Know...?

That during The Festival, there are 208 bookmakers' pitches, four permanent betting shops and three mobile betting shops?

Did You Know...?

That the second day of The Festival in 2008 was lost to exceptionally high winds? The races due to be run that day were split between the third and fourth days, with 10 races on the Thursday and nine on the Friday.

**The pictures in this book were provided
courtesy of the following:**

PA IMAGES
WWW.PRESSASSOCIATION.COM

Design and artwork by Scott Giarnese

Published by G2 Entertainment Limited

Production co-ordinator Janey Fletcher

Publishers Jules Gammond and Edward Adams

Written by Catherine Austen